Tsars, Mandarins,
and Commissars

HARRY SCHWARTZ has been a specialist in Soviet affairs and a member of the editorial board of the New York *Times* for more than twenty years. He has taught at Columbia University, Brooklyn College, New York University, and American University, and was Professor of Economics at Syracuse University from 1946 to 1953. Mr. Schwartz is the author of several books about the USSR, including *The Red Phoenix: Russia Since World War II; Russia's Soviet Economy; Russia's Postwar Economy;* and *Eastern Europe in the Soviet Shadow*.

Tsars, Mandarins, and Commissars

A History of Chinese-Russian Relations

Harry Schwartz

Revised Edition

ANCHOR BOOKS
ANCHOR PRESS/DOUBLEDAY
GARDEN CITY, NEW YORK
1973

TSARS, MANDARINS, AND COMMISSARS: A History of Chinese-Russian Relations was originally published by J. B. Lippincott Company in 1964. The Anchor Press edition is published by arrangement with Lippincott.

Anchor/Books edition: 1973

For Ruth

Preface to the Revised Edition

The publication of a new and updated edition of this book is a source of considerable gratification to this writer. When this volume first appeared in the early 1960's, its chief thesis—that the Soviet Union and the Chinese Peoples Republic were bitter enemies and that the United States could benefit by taking advantage of this rivalry—seemed incredible heresy to most people. It required almost a decade for such originally heterodox views to be implemented—and implemented brilliantly—by the Nixon Administration. Today, the reopening of direct Sino-American contacts has helped also to improve Soviet-American relations so that the world has been treated to an extraordinarily cordial meeting between President Nixon and Soviet Foreign Minister Andrei Gromyko in Washington, as well as to an equally cordial dinner meeting in New York between Secretary of State Rogers and the head of China's delegation to the United Nations General Assembly.

In the present edition, the chief change is the addition of a new last chapter which surveys Sino-Soviet relations during 1964–1972 and analyzes the impact of those relations upon the Washington-Moscow-Peking triangle. I am grateful to Stewart Richardson and Carol Goldberg of Doubleday who made this new edition possible. And, as usual, I must record my thanks to my wife, Ruth B. Schwartz, whose constant support and help made both the original version and now this updated version of this book possible.

HARRY SCHWARTZ

Scarsdale, N.Y.
October 7, 1972

Preface

This volume is an attempt to present the facts about the long history of Russian-Chinese relations in as brief and interesting a compass as possible. The effort is motivated by the belief that, for much of the period since World War II, the West in general and the United States in particular have made major mistakes in their conduct of foreign policy because of needless public ignorance about the long heritage of hate and conflict which weighs so heavily on Soviet-Chinese relations, and weighed upon it even at the height of seeming friendship and cooperation during the 1950's. The author's conviction is that this history teaches that the Sino-Soviet struggle which has so altered the political outlook of the 1960's is only secondarily an ideological struggle. Its primary components are much more nationalistic and racial distrust between Russians and Chinese, as well as competitive striving for power between the leaderships of the two countries, notably between Nikita S. Khrushchev and Mao Tse-tung. But the writer has striven—with what success only the reader can judge—to prevent his interpretation of this history from distorting his presentation of the facts of that history.

In recounting the history told here, the author has sought to give a bird's eye view of more distant periods, emphasizing general trends and key events. As the chronicle has come closer to the present, there has been more detail added to the picture. The greatest detail and the fullest account have been given about the politically shattering events of 1962 and 1963 which have ended the myth of Soviet-Chinese friendship and revealed the antagonism that was only briefly hidden by the alliance born of common dogma. This writer has sought to take into account the many major—and previously secret— revelations about Soviet-Chinese relations in the 1950's and early 1960's which were made public in the exchange of verbal broadsides Peking and Moscow hurled at each other in the summer and fall of 1963.

The writer of a volume such as this has many debts, primarily to the researchers and historians who did the spade work in earlier years to produce much of the material employed here. It is the author's regret that the need to remain within a fixed size of book and the importance of recounting the Soviet-Chinese verbal duels which continued even while this book was being set in type forced the elimination of the extensive bibliography which had been prepared. However the notes indicate some of the major sources used and name some of the key earlier writers upon whom this book has drawn.

George Stevens of J. B. Lippincott Company made possible the writing of this volume, for which the author is grateful indeed. Stewart Richardson and Lavinia Russell of the same organization helped in many ways during the writing and printing. Dr. Allen Whiting was good enough to read most of the manuscript and made helpful suggestions, though he should not be blamed for errors or for this volume's interpretations. The author's wife, Ruth B. Schwartz, did yeoman service far above and beyond the call of duty in bearing with a writer in the agonies of composition and then copy-editing this volume and preparing the index. Thanks are due to the owners of copyrighted materials quoted in this volume for giving permission to reprint these materials. All errors in this volume are the author's sole responsibility, and the New York *Times,* the author's employer, is in no way responsible for the opinions expressed here.

HARRY SCHWARTZ

Scarsdale, N.Y.
November 3, 1963

Contents

MAPS
following page xi
China, Siberia, and Soviet Central Asia
Territorial Changes Along the Russo-Chinese Border
Since 1840

China, Siberia, an

UNION O

UNION OF SOVIET SOCIALIST REPUBLICS

CHINA

PACIFIC OCEAN

Yenisei R.

Tomsk

Novosibirsk

Semipalatinsk

TA
Sa

KAZAKH S.S.R.

Lake
Balkhash

Aral
Sea

Tarbagatai

Urumchi

Kuldja

Alma-Ata

Ily
R.

Wusu

UZBEK S.S.R.

Khiva

Tashkent

Lake
Issyk-Kul
KIRGHIZ S.S.R.

Khokand

SINKIANG
(Sinkiang-Uigur
Autonomous Region

Caspian Sea

TURKMEN
S.S.R.

Samarkand

TADZHIK
S.S.R.

Kashgar

Teheran

Kabul

TIBÈT

IRAN

AFGHANISTAN

Rawalpindi

Srinagar

Himalayan M

Persian
Gulf

Gulf of
Oman

PAKISTAN

Delhi

NEPAL

Katmandu

INDIA

Arabian Sea

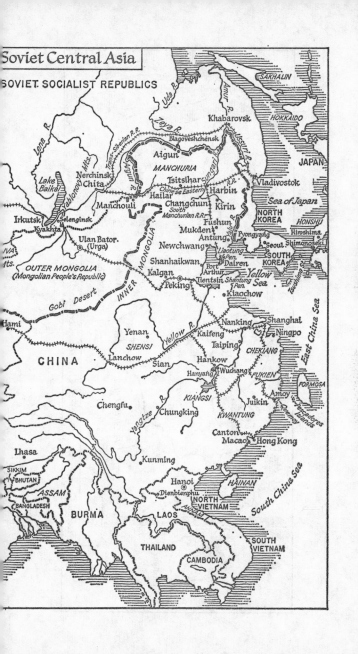

Soviet Central Asia

SOVIET SOCIALIST REPUBLICS

SAKHALIN
HOKKAIDO
Uda R.
Lena R.
Zeya R.
Khabarovsk
Amur R.
Blagoveshchensk
Aigun
Ussuri R.
Yablonovy Mts.
Trans-Siberian R.R.
MANCHURIA
JAPAN
Nerchinsk
Lake Baikal
Chita
Tsitsihar
Sungari R.
Chinese Eastern R.R.
Harbin
Vladivostok
Manchouli
Hailar
Changchun
South Manchurian R.R.
Kirin
Sea of Japan
Irkutsk
Selenginsk
Kyakhta
Fushun
Mukden
Antung
NORTH KOREA
HONSHU
Hiroshima
TUVA
Mts.
Ulan Bator (Urga)
Newchwang
Pyongyang
Seoul
Shimonoseki
OUTER MONGOLIA
(Mongolian People's Republic)
MONGOLIA
INNER
Shanhaikwan
Liaotung Pen.
Port Arthur
Dairen
SOUTH KOREA
Tsushima
Kalgan
Tientsin
Shantung Pen.
Yellow Sea
Gobi Desert
Peking
Kiaochow
Hami
Yenan
SHENSI
Yellow R.
Nanking
Shanghai
Ningpo
East China Sea
CHINA
Lanchow
Sian
Kaifeng
Taiping
CHEKIANG
Hankow
Hanyang
Wuchang
FUKIEN
FORMOSA
Chengfu
KIANGSI
Yangtze R.
Chungking
Juikin
Amoy
Pescadores Islands
KWANTUNG
Canton
Macao
Hong Kong
Lhasa
Kunming
SIKKIM
BHUTAN
ASSAM
Hanoi
Dienbienphu
HAINAN
South China Sea
BANGLADESH
BURMA
NORTH VIETNAM
LAOS
THAILAND
CAMBODIA
SOUTH VIETNAM

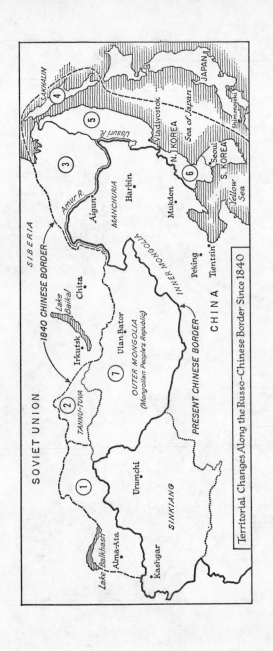

Territorial Changes Along the Russo-Chinese Border Since 1840

Tsars, Mandarins,
and Commissars

CHAPTER I

The Unnatural Alliance

Surprise and incredulity dominated the Western world in the summer of 1963 as a furious battle of words raged between the planet's two great Communist-ruled nations. On July 31, 1963, for example, the government of Communist China declared in an official statement: "The indisputable facts prove that the policy pursued by the Soviet government is one of allying with the forces of war to oppose the forces of peace, allying with imperialism to oppose Socialism, allying with the United States to oppose China, and allying with the reactionaries of all countries to oppose the people of the world." In Moscow three days later the Soviet government asserted: "The leaders of China have shown to the whole world that their policy leads to the aggravation of international tensions, to further stepping up of the arms race, to still further expansion of its scope and scale. This position is tantamount to actual connivance with those who advocate world thermonuclear war, who are against the settlement of disputable international problems at a conference table."[1]*

The shock produced by this and other bitter Sino-Soviet exchanges that summer arose because this evidence contradicted what had for many years been the most basic assumption of American policy and American public opinion about the Cold War which had raged for almost two decades since the end of World War II. This assumption

* Superior figures refer to Notes at end of text.

was the belief that the key fact of international politics was the struggle between the united forces of good against the unholy forces of evil, the former represented by the Western democracies and the latter by the Communist bloc under the leadership of the Sino-Soviet alliance. Only a few months before the public explosion of Moscow-Peking enmity, the President of the United States had warned his people against attaching any great importance to earlier signs of discord between the two great Communist giants. To President Kennedy in early 1963, the dispute had seemed merely a quarrel over tactics, a dispute over the best means of burying the free world. This view was to be proved highly erroneous by the swift march of events which followed, but it flowed naturally from the belief—nurtured by the long Cold War—that the primary world struggle was essentially a kind of religious war, a contest to determine which of two competing ideologies would rule the world. Even after the United States, Great Britain and the Soviet Union had signed a limited nuclear test ban treaty in August 1963 and reciprocal Sino-Soviet denunciations over this action had become a daily event, American officials were still warning against exaggerating the importance of the break between Moscow and Peking. It was left to French President Charles de Gaulle, representative and leader of a far older and more sophisticated civilization, to express some essential truths which had long eluded American leaders and American public opinion alike:

I will speak first on the ideological rupture, then about reality, that is the Moscow agreement [for a limited nuclear test ban]. The break? Over what ideology? During my lifetime, communist ideology has been personified by many people. There have been the eras of Lenin and Trotsky and Stalin—whom I knew personally—and of Beria and Malenkov and Khrushchev and Tito and Nagy and Mao Tse-tung. I know as many holders of the communist ideology as there are fathers of Europe. And that makes it quite a few. Each of these holders in his turn condemns, excommunicates, crushes and at times kills the others. In any event, he firmly fights against the personality cult of the others. I refuse to enter into a valid discussion of the ideological quarrel between Peking and Moscow. What I want to consider are the deep-rooted realities which are human, national and consequently international. The banner of ideology in reality covers only ambitions. And I believe that it has been thus since the world was born.[2]

It is the central thesis of this volume—a belief held by the author long before the climactic events of mid-1963— that President de Gaulle was more nearly right in July 1963 than President Kennedy had been six months earlier. The Sino-Soviet alliance was an unnatural one because the fundamental interests of those two nations were and are far more opposed than coincident. The long history of Chinese-Russian relations explored in this book provides abundant evidence of how conflicting the national interests of these two great nations have been and are. Only a widespread and needless ignorance of this history made possible the stereotyped views of the Sino-Soviet relationship which dominated United States thinking and policy during the 1950's and early 1960's.

Greater historical perspective might have enabled United States leaders and public opinion alike to understand at that time the full significance of the fateful event which occurred in Moscow on October 19, 1961. On that day a Chinese statesman, the scion of a great mandarin family, took a historic step. Rising to speak in the Kremlin before the Twenty-second Congress of the Soviet Communist party, the Premier of Communist China, Chou En-lai, declared:

We hold that if a dispute or difference unfortunately arises between fraternal parties or fraternal countries, it should be resolved patiently in the spirit of proletarian internationalism and on the principles of equality and unanimity through consultations. Any public, one-sided censure of any fraternal party does not help unity, and is not helpful in resolving problems. To lay bare a dispute between fraternal parties or fraternal countries openly in the face of the enemy cannot be regarded as a serious Marxist-Leninist attitude. Such an attitude will only grieve those near and dear to us and gladden our enemies.[3]

At first glance these words seem mild, almost platitudinous. Actually they were a public declaration by China of political war against the rulers of the Soviet Union headed by Stalin's successor, Nikita Sergeyevich Khrushchev. Chou En-lai's words were a specific, direct and open refusal to accept the public denunciation of Albania, China's first modern European satellite, which Premier Khrushchev had delivered in that same hall before that same audience two days earlier. The immediate issue was Sino-Soviet rivalry over command of Albania, but Chou En-lai chose to ignore the difference of national interests and to phrase his criticism in ideological terms. His assertion that what Khrushchev had done "cannot be regarded as a serious Marxist-Leninist attitude" was a charge that the Moscow ruler had strayed from the true faith and was now a heretic.

The most perceptive observers of the Sino-Soviet relationship recognized the historic significance of this step at the time. They realized that the Red mandarin from China had boldly challenged the Communist Tsar of Muscovy in the very center of his realm. Their minds swept back to another October some 444 years earlier, to the day when Martin Luther chose to defy the Pope of Rome by posting his 95 Theses on the door of the castle church in Wittenberg. The analogy was intriguing. The fission of Christendom initiated by Luther had powerfully shaped the history of the West for almost half a millennium. Would the fission of the Communist world revealed by Chou En-lai in the Kremlin have comparable consequences? The potentials were certainly there.

But the full significance of this event was not realized at the time by either American policy makers or American public opinion. This failure of understanding occurred because a simple syllogism, derived from the logic of the Cold War, had been at the base of most United States thinking in this area since Mao Tse-tung conquered China's mainland in the late 1940's. Here are the premises and the conclusion drawn from them:

1. All Communists want to destroy the free world and establish world Communism.
2. The Soviet Union and Communist China are Communist-ruled nations.
3. Therefore, the Soviet Union and Communist China must be united in working to destroy the free world and to establish world Communism.

We can imagine Moslem thinkers of the Middle Ages arguing in a similar vein: all Christians want to destroy Islam and establish world Christianity. The nations of Western Europe are ruled by Christians. Therefore Western Europe must be united to destroy Islam and establish world Christianity.

From our vantage point in time we know how false any such Moslem reasoning turned out to be. In reality the history of Western Europe these past several centuries is one of frequent and bloody fratricidal strife, sometimes based on religious differences within Christianity, as during the Thirty Years' War, but more often derived from differences of national interest and ambition, as in the last two world wars. Anti-Moslem crusades have been unfashionable for centuries.

The essence of the matter is that normally neither men nor nations live exclusively on the basis of religion or its modern secular analogue, ideology. And even where religion has tended to be dominant in the past, that dominion has been no guarantee of unity. Each of the world's great religions has been split time and again as the many existing varieties of Christianity, Mohammedanism, Buddhism and Judaism testify. The relationship between two nations cannot be predicted in any simple manner for very long solely on the basis of the dominant religion or ideology. Along with religion or ideology, we must look at considerations of relative power, of national interest, of historic and cultural background, of level of economic development and—not least—the attitudes and ambitions of the national leaders of a given time. Let us try to look at the Soviet Union and China today from a broader perspective than that adopted in the simplistic syllogism recited above.

The Chinese possess one of the oldest and proudest civilizations of all history, a society which was accustomed to regarding foreigners—often with justice—as barbarians. Writing in 1939, Mao Tse-tung showed that he found national pride entirely compatible with his Communist beliefs:

> In the history of Chinese civilization, agriculture and handicrafts have always been known as highly developed; many great thinkers, scientists, inventors, statesmen, military experts, men of letters, and artists have flourished, and there is a rich store of classical works. The compass was invented in China very long ago. The art of paper-making was discovered as early as 1,800 years ago. Block printing was invented 1,300 years ago. In addition, movable types were invented 800 years ago. Gunpowder was used in China earlier than in Europe. China, with a recorded history of almost 4,000 years, is therefore one of the oldest civilized countries in the world. . . .
>
> All the nationalities of China have always rebelled against the foreign yoke and striven to shake it off by means of resistance. They accept a union on the basis of equality, not the oppression of one nationality by another. In thousands of years of history of the Chinese nation many national heroes and revolutionary leaders have emerged. So the Chinese nation is also a nation with a glorious revolutionary tradition and a splendid historical heritage.[4]

Until the middle of the nineteenth century, the Chinese felt they had every reason to be satisfied with their society and its culture, both of which they thought immeasurably superior to any others. For thousands of years the dominant Han people had survived through all vicissitudes, overcoming and absorbing conqueror after conqueror through their biological vitality and the attractiveness of their civilization. That civilization had been formed on the basis of ideas quite foreign to the West. In Confucius, Mo Tzu, Lao Tzu and other great shapers of their tradition, the Chinese felt they had great thinkers and exemplars without rival elsewhere. When Buddhism penetrated China almost 2,000 years ago, it was quickly absorbed and transformed, adding to and modifying the traditional Chinese philosophy and world outlook rather than ousting them. Christianity has had only peripheral and most superficial effects upon Chinese thinking, far less even than the minor impact of the Moslem religion which was adopted by some relatively small groups of Chinese subjects. China's self-satisfaction and high appreciation of its culture are best attested by the fact that for centuries the country was ruled under the Emperor by the mandarin bureaucracy whose members were selected and promoted on the basis of their performance on examinations testing their knowledge of the classical Chinese writings.

To the Chinese, their country traditionally was the Middle Kingdom, the head of a family of nations that included Japan, Siam, Korea, Annam and Burma. China, as the senior, had the responsibility for maintaining order within this family and coming to the aid of members when trouble struck. The other states were tributaries whose submission was shown by the periodic sending of envoys who performed the traditional *kowtow* before the Emperor, kneeling three times and knocking the head on the floor nine times. An envoy brought tribute to the Emperor and was allowed to sell goods from his own country which he had been permitted to bring with him duty-free. In turn, the Emperor gave the envoy, his retainers and the vassal king he represented rich gifts, presents often more valuable than those he had brought. All this was a far cry from the Western concept of equality between states.

The Chinese Emperor claimed to be the Son of Heaven and ruler of all the world. The Book of Odes declared: "Under the wide heaven, there is no land that is not the Emperor's, and within the sea boundary of the land, there is none who is not a subject of the Emperor." The Emperor and his people regarded as barbarians all who did not accept Chinese civilization and culture. As Professor Hsü has put it: "In their utter ignorance of the beauty of the Chinese way of life and in their lack of sufficient intellect to appreciate reason and ethics, the barbarians were considered no different from the lower animals." The duty of the Emperor was to help civilize the barbarians, to chastise them if need be and to guard the Empire against possible attack by the barbarians. When Russia and China first met, therefore, and for many decades afterward, it seemed to the men in Peking that they had encountered a new tribe of barbarians, one to which the precedents of the past could properly be applied.[5] Similar thinking was applied to the other Western nations, as well, in the early phases of China's contacts with them. Perhaps the most generous Chinese comment about Europeans before the nineteenth century was the assertion that while the Chinese alone had two eyes, the Franks (that is, the Western Europeans) were one-eyed and all of the earth's other peoples were blind.[6]

The rude and successful intrusion of the West into China in the nineteenth century shattered this complacency as it quickly became evident that neither Chinese philosophy nor its ancient military lore were adequate to stand up to the military technology these new "barbarian" invaders possessed. But the ancient pride was still strong, expressed even in this typical reform program presented by a high official, Feng Kuei-fen, in the mid-nineteenth century:

We have only one thing to learn from the barbarians, and that is strong ships and effective guns. . . . Funds should be allotted to establish a shipyard and arsenal in each trading port. A few barbarians should be employed and Chinese who are good in using their minds should be selected to receive instruction so that in turn they may teach many craftsmen. . . .

The intelligence and ingenuity of the Chinese are certainly superior to those of the various barbarians; it is only that hitherto we have not made use of them. . . . There ought to be some people of extraordinary intelligence who can have new ideas and improve on Western methods. At first they may take the foreigners as their teachers and models; then they may come to the same level and be their equals; finally they may move ahead and surpass them. Herein lies the way to self-strengthening.[7]

Feng concluded his prescription with the exhortation that "the way to avoid trouble is to manufacture, repair, and use weapons by ourselves. Only thus can we pacify the empire; only thus can we become the leading power in the world; only thus can we restore our original strength, redeem ourselves from former humiliations, and maintain the integrity of our vast territory so as to remain the greatest country on earth." The words are worth remembering now, a century later.

From the point of view of China's present Communist rulers, Feng's advice was wrong because it overlooked the need to import a Western ideology, Marxism-Leninism, to revitalize the nation. The break with the older tradition implied thereby is clear, but it should not be over-emphasized. The Chinese ability to modify and absorb imported doctrines has been shown before, and the ideological debates of the early 1960's have already demonstrated that Peking's understanding of Marxism-Leninism is by no means identical with the concept of that doctrine held further west.

It has been fashionable at times in the past to emphasize Russia's Asiatic heritage. The two centuries of Mongol domination and their aftereffects, both biological and cultural, are most often cited in this connection, along with the fact that Russia experienced neither the Reformation nor the Renaissance, which so powerfully molded Western and Central Europe.

But in comparison with China can there be any doubt that Russia belongs to the West biologically, culturally and historically? Russians, Ukrainians and Belorussians, who together make up some three-quarters of the Soviet population, are white men, the eastern representatives of the great Slavic linguistic branch of humanity whose western cousins are such unquestionably European peoples as the Poles, the Czechs and the Serbs. It was almost a thousand years ago, in 988, that Vladimir, ruler of Kievan Rus, abandoned paganism for Christianity and made the Orthodox variety of this creed the dominant religion of Russia. Vladimir Monomakh, Grand Prince of Kiev from 1113 to 1125, had an Englishman's daughter as his wife. A century earlier his great predecessor Yaroslav had sired daughters who became queens of France, Hungary and Norway.

When Russia reformed under Muscovite leadership, ended Mongol dominion and began the expansion which brought it to its present borders, it was to the West that its rulers looked for ideas and technology. Peter the Great's services in reknitting the weakened ties with the West at the end of the seventeenth century and the first quarter of the eighteenth are too well known to need repetition. The intellectual giants of Western Europe were frequent and welcome guests at the court of Catherine the Great. Many a nineteenth century Russian nobleman spoke French more fluently than his native language. Napoleon was defeated by General Winter in Russia but the ideas of the French Revolution contributed much to the ferment in Russia during the last century of Romanov rule. And has anyone ever questioned that Pushkin, Tolstoy, Tschaikovsky, Glinka, Lobachevsky and Mechnikov belong to the main stream of western culture and science?

Most important for our present purpose is the strain of imperialism and expansionism which has been present in much Russian thinking these past 500 years. One aspect of this was enunciated by the monk Filofei a few decades after the fall of Constantinople. The original Rome had fallen to the barbarians, he declared, because it had lapsed into heresy. Constantinople had become the second Rome and had succumbed because of the same error. Now Moscow had become the third capital of the world, the third Rome. As subsequent developments were to show, many who came after Filofei shared his vision of Moscow's role in the world, even though they started from other assumptions. The great non-Communist Russian philosopher Nikolai Berdyayev wrote in the 1930's:

> The Russian people have not realized their messianic idea of Moscow the Third Rome. . . . Instead of the Third Rome in Russia, the Third International was achieved and many of the features of the Third Rome were transferred to the Third International. The fact that the Third International is not international but a Russian national idea is very poorly understood in the West. Here we have the transformation of Russian messianism. Western communists, when they join the Third International, do not understand that in joining the Third International they are joining the Russian people and helping to realize its messianic vocation.[8]

In China and Russia we have two very different peoples. One nation consists of men and women with what we call yellow skins; the other mainly of people whose skin colors we loosely lump together as white. Both are proud peoples and each has within its tradition ideas of racial and national superiority which are in their nature mutually incompatible. The Marxism-Leninism that united them during the 1950's and early 1960's was a recent accretion of both peoples, added to very different cultures, histories and world views. This was hardly the most auspicious background for a relationship of warm mutual confidence and trust. Perhaps what should surprise us is not that discord finally broke out into the open, but that the public façade of full unanimity and unmarred friendship could be kept up for as long as it was.

Adding to these differences of background is the vast

gulf in economic development that now separates the Soviet Union and Communist China. Russia laid the foundation for modern industry and science more than half a century before the American Revolution. China did not begin to face up to the need for laying such foundations until about the time of the American Civil War. Tsarist Russia in 1913 was much more developed industrially and technically than was the China of 1950, while the average standard of living of the Russian peasant or worker in 1913 was well above anything which has yet been achieved in Communist China in the mid-1960's.

Today the Soviet Union, while probing the planets with its rockets, measures its economic and scientific strength boldly against that of the United States and dreams of achieving Utopian abundance by 1980. The China of today is a vast sink of poverty, dependent mainly upon the power of human muscles. And the Chinese state is still not in a position to assure its people a ration of rice adequate for their strength and health. Russia today is relatively far richer in comparison to China than the United States is in comparison to the Soviet Union.

The rich man in his mansion does not usually see eye to eye with the beggar in his hovel, nor do the two usually feel any great common interest. This comparison may be helpful in understanding the relationship between Moscow's relatively affluent society and Peking's stag-geringly poor society. The Chinese would be inhumanly virtuous if this obvious contrast did not excite their envy. Their resentment at what they consider Russia's miser-liness in extending economic aid to China is suggested by more than a little evidence. The men in Moscow would be incredibly naive if they did not worry about the possibility of future threats to their relative prosperity from China. We know, of course, that the men in Moscow are not naive and have thought about these problems. In private conversations Premier Khrushchev and lower ranking Soviet officials have spoken openly of their concern. And concerned they may well be, for Russia has one-third China's population on a territory almost three times as large. May not a China of the future demand a more equitable sharing of *lebensraum* and natural resources between the "brotherly Soviet and Chinese peoples"? No more reassuring to Moscow are the population projections which forecast that the 700,000,000 Chinese of today may increase to more than 1,500,000,000 souls by the year 2000. The year 2000, it should be added, is fewer years away than the years which have passed since Lenin's death in 1924.

The problem involved here, of course, is not Russia's alone. In the long run China's leaders—Communists or not—will surely demand a more equitable share of the entire world's resources, one giving their prolific people a "fairer portion" of the earth's land and other bounty than has been produced by the workings of history to date. From a Chinese point of view, the "injustice" of America's vast wealth spread among a people less than one-third as numerous as China's must seem even more flagrant than the Soviet good fortune. But the United States is a long way off on the other side of the vast Pacific Ocean. Russia with its long common border separating relatively empty and extremely rich Siberia from crowded China is literally next door.

What adds sharpness and urgency to these considerations, of course, is the long history of Soviet-Chinese disputes. As we shall see below, these stretch back at least to the middle of the seventeenth century, but the main discord to date has been concentrated in the period since 1850. Korea, Manchuria, Mongolia and Sinkiang have all been areas of bitter rivalry, while much of the present Soviet Far East was wrested from China by Russia only as recently as 1858–1860. A century is not long in the history of the Chinese nation, which prides itself on records stretching back four millennia. We need not wonder, therefore, that in early 1963 Communist China reminded Communist Russia that it had not forgotten the nineteenth century Muscovite imperialist forays against the hapless Manchu Empire. India has learned to its sorrow how seriously Communist China takes its border

claims. Will the same lesson be taught Russia some day?
The men in Moscow can only wonder, and prepare for
the worst.

Before beginning our detailed discussion of the history
of Russian-Chinese relations, a few words on the borderlands between the two nations may be helpful.

During the past several centuries, Russia and China
have faced each other across a border stretching many
thousands of miles, but breaking down naturally into three
sectors. Proceeding from west to east, these three sectors
are: the long boundary from the southwest to the northeast which separates Soviet Central Asia from Sinkiang
(an area also known as Chinese Turkestan and, most recently, as the Sinkiang-Uigur Autonomous Region); then
the long demarcation line drawn roughly due west to east
separating Siberia from what used to be known as Outer
Mongolia, now the independent Mongolian Peoples Republic; and finally the roughly crescent-shaped Far Eastern boundary—along the Amur River and its tributaries,
the Argun and the Ussuri—which separates the Soviet Far
East from Manchuria. The history of each of these boundaries—how it came into being, how it was altered and how
its attempted alteration was frustrated at times—is a semi-
separate story, since disputes and intrigues in one border
area were often independent of developments elsewhere.
This factor explains some of the complexity of the history
recounted in this volume.

Much of the traditional Russian-Chinese boundary passes
through difficult and unattractive country, often moun-
tainous or desert-like in character and subject to extremes
of heat and cold. On both sides of this vast boundary,
comparatively few people lived in these borderlands before the twentieth century. Even as late as 1900 there were
very few Han people—the basic group we call Chinese—
among the inhabitants of China's border areas. In Sinkiang,
the Moslem peoples had and have close historical, cultural
and religious ties with the similar groups farther west in
Soviet Central Asia. The political importance of that fact

was underlined in September 1963 when the Peking regime revealed that tens of thousands of Sinkiang's inhabitants had fled across the border to Soviet territory in early 1962. The Mongols in Outer Mongolia were and are a comparatively small group spread over a vast area— much of it desert and poor pastureland. They are related historically and culturally both to the Mongols of China's Inner Mongolia and to some of the peoples of Siberia. The sensitivity of this division of the Mongols was vividly revealed in 1962 when the rulers of Outer Mongolia, with Soviet support, purged a high official on grounds he sought to glorify and exalt the memory of Genghis Kahn. At the same time, in China's Inner Mongolia, Genghis Khan was being praised as a progressive figure in history, one whose conquests almost a millennium earlier had served the cause of mankind's advance. Finally we come to Manchuria—the original home of the last Chinese dynasty, that of the Manchu Emperors. During much of their rule over China, the Manchus sought to keep Manchuria sparsely settled and free of Chinese colonization.

On the Russian side of the border, as of 1900, the number of ethnic Russians living in Central Asia and Siberia was small. In many parts of these areas, Russians were greatly outnumbered by non-Russians. Siberia, we may recall, was for many decades a limbo to which political dissidents and criminals were exiled, though some bolder spirits among the peasantry came voluntarily, encouraged often by government subsidy and help. The conquered Moslem peoples of Central Asia—dreaming often of independence and of union with other Moslems— posed and still pose delicate political problems for the rulers of the Soviet Union. These geographic, political, ethnic and demographic factors have all played a role in determining the decisions taken by both sides in the numerous Russian-Chinese confrontations across the border, as well as in influencing the outcome of these confrontations.

CHAPTER II

The Road to Nerchinsk

In the middle of the sixteenth century, long after the discovery of America, the government of Ivan the Terrible had little knowledge of China. When the bold British adventurer Antony Jenkinson came to Moscow in the 1550's to begin his search for an overland route to China for the Muscovy Company, he got permission to traverse the Tsar's realm toward his goal, but little information. In the 1580's the Moscow regime sent emissaries to Siberia. They sought answers to questions that were put this way: "Where is the Chinese state? How rich is it? Is there anything we can get from it?"

But there had been earlier contacts between Russians and Chinese, many of them. Russia and China, after all, had been parts of the great Mongol empire at its height in the late thirteenth century. Russian princes such as Alexander Nevsky, who traveled to the Grand Khan's court in Karakorum to receive their *yarlik*, or patent of rule, must have met Chinese, many of whom played prominent roles at the court of the Mongol rulers. Kublai Khan—he whom Marco Polo observed and served—used thousands of drafted Russian soldiers when he began his major campaign to conquer South China in 1267. In the 1330's the Grand Khan's capital was in Peking and one of its military forces was a special Russian division stationed nearby. The Russians were settled on lands north of Peking and supplied with clothes, oxen, tools and seeds. Their obligation was to supply the imperial table with all the different kinds of game and fish which abounded in the area's forests, rivers and lakes. Thousands of Russian captives were enslaved and sent to Peking to serve the khan. Centuries later, when the first Russian envoys arrived in Peking to begin the modern history of Sino-Russian relations, they found much in the etiquette of the Chinese court which reminded them of the Tsar's court in Moscow, more evidence of the impact of the common Mongol rule.

Memories of the contacts with China during the Mongol era may have been dim or non-existent in sixteenth century Russia, but the memory of the Mongol rule itself has never been eradicated from Russian national memory. The belief grew in later centuries that Russia's backwardness compared to the West was the price of Russian heroism in protecting the ungrateful West from the warriors of the khans. The great Russian poet Aleksander Blok put it this way in his famous poem, *The Scythians:*[1]

> Centuries of your days are but an hour to us,
> Yet like obedient guards
> We've held a shield between two hostile races:
> Europe, and the Mongol hordes.

Blok calls on Europeans to join Russians as friends, putting the alternative in these graphic terms:

> But we, we will no longer shield you
> Nor fight at all,
> Content observing with our narrow eyes
> The death brew boil.

> Nor shall we flinch to see the ferocious Hun
> Pillage each corpse,
> Herd all his horses into church and burn
> Mounds of white flesh.

> Ah, Old World, before you have perished, join
> Our fraternal banquet. Hear
> Perhaps for the last time summoning you
> The barbaric lyre!

The argument Blok put forward in his poem is one that has been made in prose more than once these past few years by Russians conversing privately with Western friends. Now, of course, it is the Chinese hordes they have in mind.

China and Russia first faced each other as antagonists across a disputed border in the 1650's. The confrontation took place less than a decade after the Manchu dynasty had taken power in Peking. It was an inevitable byproduct of the remarkable burst of energy which brought Russian dominion over much of northern Asia during the late sixteenth and early seventeenth centuries. The secret of that remarkable expansion was stated succinctly much later by Dostoyevsky when he declared: "In Europe we were hangers-on and slaves, whereas we shall go to Asia as masters. In Europe we were Asiatics, whereas in Asia we, too, are Europeans."[2] The small, poor and primitive peoples who inhabited Siberia were far more backward even than the subjects of Ivan the Terrible and the early Romanovs. These weak and disunited tribes had even less chance to stop the Russian conquest than had—thousands of miles away—the far more highly civilized Aztecs and Incas of stopping the Spaniards under Cortez and Pizarro. The Russian with the gun was the military master of the dark-skinned native with primitive weapons and inferior military organization.

It was a motley crew indeed that conquered Siberia for the Russian Tsar, and only handfuls of men were involved in the initial conquests. Vast areas were seized for Moscow by bands of adventurers numbering only tens or hundreds of individuals. The great Russian merchant family, the Stroganovs, provided much of the initial impetus and financing for the great push eastward. The men who actually explored and conquered Siberia were mainly Cossack freebooters, runaway serfs, vagrants and other refugees from the ordered hierarchical society of the Tsar. Their small groups traveled eastward, usually following the great river systems of Siberia initially and then spreading out along the tributary streams. They fought battles as the need arose, withstood the rigors of Siberia's extreme cold and almost as extreme heat, and overcame hunger and disease. To buttress their power, they built rude forts at strategic points from which they ruled the natives, forced them to swear allegiance to the Tsar and collected tributes of furs and provisions. Greed, the desire for adventure and fear of what would happen to them if they returned to Old Russia drove these men on across the vast distances. Rabble and cutthroats they may have seemed to the Tsar and his court, but they brought Russia a vast domain whose full potentials still remain to be realized in the future. The bulk of this vast work of exploration and conquest took place between 1582 and 1639. By the latter year Russians had reached the Pacific. A new era of history had been opened, but few men of the time realized the enormous significance of the event.

This easy and rapid expansion into a power vacuum stopped only when the Russian force collided with another power of comparable strength, the Chinese under the direction of the Manchus. To the Chinese and their rulers the Russians were barbarians, fit only to be tribute-paying subjects of the Emperor if that could be accomplished. It took decades before the Chinese court was willing to treat with the Russians on an equal basis. To the crude but vigorous and expansion-minded Russians, the strength of the new antagonist came as an unwelcome shock, but the riches of the Chinese empire stimulated thoughts of gains from trade and even richer gains from future conquest. The strength of Russian imperialist aspirations and feelings of superiority is suggested by this extract from a poem by Gavrila Derzhavin, the eighteenth century predecessor of Pushkin, who praised the ideal reign of Catherine II and expressed the hope that

> Peoples savage and remote
> Covered still with wool and scales,
> Dressed only with leaf and bark,
> And adorned with wings of birds,

Should all gather at her throne,
Hear the gentle voice of Law,
So that tears should run in torrents
Down their swarthy sunburned faces.
They should cry and understand
The bliss of living in our time,
Should abandon their equality
And all subject be to Her.[3]

It was through Mongolia that the first modern direct
contact between Moscow and Peking took place. As the
Russians moved into this area in the early 1600's and
communicated with the nomadic and semi-nomadic peoples there, they learned of a great and rich civilization far
to the southeast. Here is the way *Voyevod* Volynsky put
the astonishing news in a message to the Tsar in 1608:

Beyond the land of Altyn Khan of the Mongols, three
months travel away, is the country of Kitai. Here there
are towns built of stone, and dwellings such as are found
in Moscow. The Tsar of Kitai is stronger and richer
than the Altyn Khan. There are many churches in the
town with bells that ring. But these churches are without crosses and we do not know of what religion they
are. The people live like Russians, they possess weapons,
and they trade with different countries from which they
obtain precious objects from all parts of the world.[4]

The news was fascinating and intriguing; it raised rich
perspectives for the future, though it may have brought
forebodings to some far-sighted men. But more information was needed. In 1618 the *voyevod* of Tomsk, Prince
Kurakin, decided to send a mission directly to Peking. He
chose the Cossacks Ivan Petlin and Peter Kozylov. They
must have been brave and hardy men for they reached
their destination following a path that can be approxi-
mately marked on a modern map through the cities Tomsk-
Kuznetsk-Ulan Bator-Kalgan-Peking. The envoys received
a message from the Chinese Emperor indicating his willingness to trade with the Russians, and they brought it back to

the Siberian city of Tobolsk. But since no one in Tobolsk could read the language of the message it lay in the archives there for more than half a century before being translated into Russian.

The Petlin-Kozylov mission thus had no practical results. But as the seventeenth century wore on, the two nations' knowledge about each other increased. Moreover, their direct and indirect contracts became more frequent. In Mongolia itself there was sharp rivalry as the Russians and the Manchus intrigued to extend their sway over this vast area. In 1634 the Russians scored a diplomatic *coup* when they induced the Mongol Altyn Khan to sign a document acknowledging himself a vassal of the Tsar. The Mongols became trade intermediaries between Russia and China. Their caravans brought Chinese silks, silver and other goods to Tomsk. It is a measure of the Russians' continued ignorance about China that the trade records for Tomsk for such years as 1640, 1652 and 1653 give no indication of Chinese goods being received there. A Russian chronicler explains that at the time even silk cloth was not regarded as a Chinese product in Russia.[5] But the real Russian-Chinese confrontation came in the second half of the seventeenth century, when the Russians went far beyond Lake Baikal and began to settle along the Amur River in what is now the Soviet Far East.

The Russians arrived in the Amur River Basin almost simultaneously with the Manchu conquest of China, in particular the Manchu capture of Peking in 1644. An expedition headed by Vasily Poyarkov left Yakutsk in 1643 and reached the Amur Basin after crossing the Stanovoi Mountains. They went from the Zeya River to the Amur and explored the latter to its mouth in the Pacific. When Poyarkov finally managed to return to Yakutsk in 1646, he brought back many valuable furs and a detailed description and maps of the territories and rivers he had traversed. A Cossack *ataman,* Yerofei Pavlovich Khabarov (the modern city of Khabarovsk is named after him), began the job of Russian colonization in this new area, dreaming of a Russian peasant paradise in the fruitful land that had been discovered. He took 70 men from Yakutsk on his first expedition in 1649, and then brought several hundred more in 1651. They founded a number of small towns, notably Albazin, and Russian farmers and hunters began to spread along the Amur. The local Daur people were easily defeated when they tried to resist this colonization; their arrows were no match for Khabarov's muskets and cannon. But behind the Daurs, the Achans and other native peoples were the Manchus, who had noted the Russian arrival with great uneasiness and who were determined to defend what they regarded as their domain. And the Manchus had some guns and cannons comparable to those the Russian freebooters possessed.

The first battle between Russians and troops of the Chinese empire took place at the mouth of the Ussuri River in 1652. Some 2,000 Manchu troops attacked the Russian fort there and at first won the upper hand. But, according to the Russian account, a desperate Cossack counterattack sent the Manchus fleeing in disorder after hundreds of their troops had been killed. If the Russian account is true, the Russians won this first battle. But the Cossacks gave up the fort and retreated, apparently fearing further attacks.

This battle of Achansky Gorod and the date it began, March 24, 1652, do not loom large in military history. By modern standards it was a mere skirmish. But symbolically it was a major milestone in the history of Asia. The Russian effort to seize more territory had met its first Chinese resistance. The results of the clash itself were indecisive, but a pattern had been set for the centuries ahead.

The significance of this first clash was not lost on Moscow. It decided to send an envoy to China to try to negotiate the border disputes and also to get an agreement for trade between the two countries. His instructions also included the injunction "to learn secretly the Chinese military strength, and all the routes into the country; and to acquire information on the customs, population, financial condition and economic wealth of the country."[6] The man chosen as envoy was a nobleman, Fyedor Isakovich Baikov. He was given 50,000 rubles from the Tsar's treasury and instructed to buy goods in Russia for resale in China. He left Moscow in 1653 and reached Peking in March 1656, bringing Russian leathers, furs and diamonds with him. Baikov had a hard time in Peking. The Chinese, determined to have Russia's inferiority acknowledged, demanded that Baikov *kowtow* to the Emperor and give the Tsar's message to a subordinate official rather than to the Emperor directly. Baikov regarded these conditions as insulting and refused to accede to them. He did not see the Emperor, as a result, but he did sell his goods at a profit before he departed in 1658. When he returned, he brought much valuable information. Even before Baikov had returned to Moscow, a second mission headed by one Perfilyev departed from Moscow in 1658 with instructions both to negotiate and trade. Perfilyev was received more hospitably in Peking when he arrived in 1660, and an exchange of presents between the Tsar and the Emperor took place. But the Chinese felt that the letter Perfilyev brought was lacking in respect and refused to make any diplomatic agreements with him.

Even while these diplomatic efforts were being made, however, clashes between Russian and Chinese forces continued in the Amur River Valley during the 1650's. Moscow sent out a regular force of troops, several thousand in number, to this region. The intention was to lay the basis for permanent occupation regardless of what the Chinese might do. But the plans to build forts and gather provisions for an even larger force of troops to come later miscarried. This Army of the Amur dwindled in size and strength as its ranks were thinned by cold, desertion and disease, and as much of its supplies and equipment was stolen. In 1654 what remained of this army went down the Sungari River under the command of Onufrei Stepanov and fought a major engagement with a Manchu fleet. Stepanov lost some of his boats and much of his artillery and supplies as well as many of his men in this battle. He decided to retreat and go into winter quarters at the mouth of the Kamara River where a fort, Kamarskoy Ostrog, was built. In March 1655 a large and well equipped Chinese force assailed the fort. The Chinese attacked vigorously for three weeks and several times came close to breaking into the fort, but at last they withdrew, apparently for lack of provisions. His forces greatly depleted by battle losses and disease, Stepanov now settled down to several years of freebooting activity, forcing the natives to give him furs and such food as they had. The Manchus decided to try to expel the invaders by starving them out, instructing the natives to leave their homes and cease cultivating crops. Stepanov tried to go on the offensive in 1658 and sailed down the Sungari again. This time the Manchus were well prepared and waited for him with a warfleet of some 47 boats, far stronger than Stepanov's force. The battle was soon over and the Chinese gained a clear-cut victory. Two years later, in 1660, the Manchus under Bahai defeated another Russian force under *Voyevod* Pashkov at Kufatan village. For the time being at least, Russian expansion had been halted by Chinese military power.

But the Amur region remained free of Russians only briefly. In the 1660's new Russian settlers and troops arrived and built forts and towns. This led to sporadic but indecisive fighting. The irritation to Russian-Chinese relations this produced was intensified when the Russians gave refuge to a native noble, the Tungus prince Gantimur, and his tribe. Gantimur had occupied a high military post under the Manchus and helped them in their earlier battles against the Russians. The Manchus demanded repeatedly that he be returned and were embittered when the Russians stalled under one pretext after another.

In the course of the negotiations over Gantimur, an incident occurred which casts a revealing light on the psychology and aspirations of these early Russians on the Amur. This was the dispatch to Peking by the *voyevod* of Nerchinsk, Danilo Arshinsky, of a document demanding that the proud Chinese Emperor become a subject of the Tsar. Here is the text of this extraordinary demand:

The Great Soverign, Tsar and Grand Duke Alexei Mi-
khailovich, Autocrat of all of Great, Little, and White
Russia, Master of numerous states, already retains under his supreme control several tsars and kings and their
states, to whom His Majesty the Tsar grants favors and
lends assistance. The Bogdoi Khan [Emperor of China]
would do well likewise to beg for the protection of His
Majesty the Tsar . . . and to become a *protégé* under
his supreme control. The Great Sovereign, Tsar, etc.,
then would lavish his favors on Bogdoi Khan, grant him
his imperial protection, and defend him against all enemies. And the Bogdoi Khan, himself forever protected
under the supreme control of His Majesty the Tsar,
would pay a tribute to the Great Sovereign, while his subjects would trade freely with the Tsar's subjects to the
profit of both states.[7]

The sheer insolence of the demand takes the breath away,
especially when one remembers that it was addressed to
the head of an empire which traditionally considered itself
natural master of all nations. Presumably Ignaty Milova-
nov, the envoy who brought this message, had the good
sense when in Peking to see that his demand did not reach
Chinese eyes. His life would almost certainly have been
forfeit had the Emperor known of this presumption.

The importance of the Gantimur incident—which dis-
turbed Sino-Russian relations for two decades—arose from
the competition between the two powers for the allegiance
of the native peoples in the areas where the two empires
were meeting. The ability of Gantimur and other refugees
to escape Manchu vassalage by receiving Russian protection was a blow to the prestige and power of the Chinese
rulers. The political and propaganda importance of this
blow was fully appreciated by each side. In the end the
Russians won; Gantimur, who became a convert to Christianity, was not returned.

Moscow in the mid-1670's was in no hurry to settle
either the border or the refugee problems. It did not have
the power in the area to impose settlements of its own.
Moreover, there were differences of opinion among the

Russians, some urging efforts to push forward rapidly
against the Chinese and others urging a more cautious
policy. Yuri Krizhanich, a representative of the latter
school, warned against adventurism here, writing: "Only
our enemies are interested in turning us away from realiz-
able undertakings and to push us on to things impossible to
carry out. Should the Russian people plunge into a stupid
war with China, the Germans and the Turks will take
advantage of the opportunity and seize the Russian state."
The Russians therefore stalled on the question of Gantimur's return, pleading one pretext after another to explain
why they could not return him. But finally Nikolai Gav-
rilovich Spathari, a Greek by origin, was sent from Moscow to the Manchu court in 1675. A recent Russian
writer has complained in these terms of Spathari's recep-
tion in Peking:

Spathari's negotiations with the Manchu mandarins met
with great difficulties. The mandarins demanded the
execution of degrading ceremonies, showed arrogance
and disrespect to the envoy, and finally established a
prison regimen for the members of the mission. Russian merchants arriving with the mission were forbidden
to communicate with Chinese merchants and they were
allowed to buy Chinese goods only in one specially set
up store. The Manchus set up fixed, artificially low
prices for the Russian goods brought along with the mission, and Chinese merchants violating this trading proce-
dure were mercilessly punished.[8]

Other sources make it clear the matter was more complex. On the basic issue, Spathari won. This was the Russian demand that dealings between the two countries be on
a basis of equality. The symbol of this victory was the fact
that Spathari was not required to *kowtow* when he met the
Emperor. The sensitivity of the issue is evidenced by the
fact that the official court bulletin put out a version of the
negotiations which was far from the actuality. According
to this:

The White Khan of Russia sent his subject Nikolai Gambriolovich [sic] with tribute of local articles. His presentation was to the effect that Russia lay far away in remote obscurity; that from ancient times there had been no relations with China; that he [the Tsar] was ignorant of Chinese letters and unacquainted with the proper style of address, that he now inclined toward civilization, expressed his devotion, and was desirous to open tribute relations.[9]

Such limited success as Spathari achieved on his mission was due to his contact with the Jesuits who served the Chinese Emperor as mathematicians, astronomers and, in this case, as translators. One of these Jesuits, Father Verbiest, became a close confidant of Spathari and the two men planned together the Russian approach to the Emperor. As a result, at this key early diplomatic negotiation between Russia and China, Latin became the common language of communication. Spathari's note to the Emperor, in Latin, asked the Manchu ruler to send an envoy to Moscow, to permit free travel of merchants between the two countries, to permit an annual exchange of Russian goods for Chinese silver, to permit precious stones to be send to Russia and to permit skilled Chinese craftsmen to migrate to Russia. Of the border questions and Gantimur there was no mention.

Not unnaturally, this communication displeased the Chinese court, which was not interested in mere matters of trade. The Chinese answer made three points. Complaining of the past futile attempts to regain Gantimur, the Chinese reply demanded the Tungus prince be sent to Peking with a Russian ambassador. It called for this ambassador to be a reasonable man who would perform the customary ritual at the Chinese court, and it demanded that peace be established on the border. These were the Chinese conditions for good relations with Russia. If they were not fulfilled, the mandarins threatened, Chinese armies would wipe out the Russian settlements and forts on the Amur. After three and a half months in Peking, Spathari was forced to leave.

In the early 1680's Peking moved to solve the problem of the border. It was anxious for a resolution because it was preparing for war against the Western Mongols and did not want to become involved in simultaneous conflict on two fronts against two foes. Two steps were therefore taken. One was the dispatch by the Emperor of a letter to the commander of the Russian base at Albazin demanding that he give up the city and leave the Amur. In what may have been a bit of psychological warfare, the Emperor promised to treat the Russians leniently and offered them the opportunity to serve in his forces if they wished. More important were the moves made to get ready for military action. High Chinese officials were sent to the Amur region to scout the situation and also to begin building ships and gathering supplies for a large, well trained army. Skirmishes were renewed; orders were given to destroy all food supplies in the area of operations in an effort to starve out the Russians, and the systematic destruction of the Russian forts on the Amur was begun. Finally the town of Albazin was isolated. In June 1685 the Chinese under General Peng Chen attacked. After a few days' resistance the defenders sued for peace. Most of the remaining Russians were allowed to leave with their arms for the Russian base at Nerchinsk; a few enlisted with the Chinese forces. Albazin itself was destroyed.

Later in 1685 the Russians returned to Albazin and built an even stronger fort there. At about the same time the Manchu Emperor sent a letter to Moscow, using two Russians as messengers, demanding that the Tsar's forces leave the Amur region and thus remove the main hindrance to peace and friendship between Russia and China. Before a reply could be received from Moscow, the Chinese forces attacked Albazin again, in July 1686. The much smaller Cossack force fought well and bravely, and the Manchus had to retire from their siege at the onset of winter. In November 1686 Peking received word from Moscow that the Russians were willing to negotiate. The peace party in Peking persuaded the Emperor to accept the idea of negotiations, and a renewed Manchu attack on

Albazin was ordered halted when the small remaining force of defenders was almost defeated. Thus, in the spring of 1687 the sporadic Russian-Chinese war on the Amur which had lasted for a quarter of a century came to an end.

Negotiations finally took place in 1689 at Nerchinsk. Russia was represented by Fyedor Alekseyevich Golovin, a former tutor of Peter the Great. He was esteemed by Peter as something of an expert on China, and he insisted that great time and expense be taken to assure that he had a properly colorful and impressive costume and trappings with which to meet the Chinese. When he finally arrived in the Amur region he was accompanied by some 2,000 soldiers, diplomats, scribes and serving people. But the Chinese delegation which arrived for the negotiations was far larger, grander, more impressive and—what was to prove decisive at key points in the negotiations—it had many more soldiers. The Chinese party headed by Prince San-go-tu is estimated to have numbered 15,000. The negotiations began with both sides presenting exaggerated demands. The Chinese delegation suggested the boundary between the two countries be set in the neighborhood of Lake Baikal and the Lena River, arguing that the area east of this had belonged to Mongols who were vassals of China. Golovin for his part called for the Amur River to be fixed as the boundary. As the negotiations proceeded, relations between the two sides grew very tense. The Jesuit Fathers Gerbillion and Pereira, who had come as translators, exerted themselves in the role of intermediaries seeking to bring the two sides together, but finally the Manchu prince threatened that if his concessions were not accepted his superior forces would attack both Nerchinsk and Albazin. Faced with this threat, Golovin moderated his position and a compromise agreement, the Treaty of Nerchinsk, was signed on August 27, 1689. The first major chapter in the history of Russian-Chinese relations thus came to an end with a document which was the first treaty between China and any European power. The official text of the treaty was in Latin and this was the only copy signed by both plenipotentiaries.

The Treaty of Nerchinsk recognized Chinese rule over most of the Amur Basin. It had six clauses. The first two defined the common boundary, which was fixed at the Argun River and from that along the Amur to south of the Kerbi River, a tributary of the Amur. Then the boundary was set at the ridge of the Yablonovy and Stanovoi Mountains whose southern slopes and whose rivers running into the Amur were defined as Chinese territory. No boundary was set in the Uda River Valley and this was left for future delimitation. The third clause provided for demolition of the Russian town of Albazin, and for all of its people and property to be moved to Russian territory. All refugees who had fled from either side earlier were to be allowed to remain where they were, but all future refugees would be handed back to the authorities of the country they had come from. Clause Five provided for free travel between the two countries by their citizens having proper passports and wishing to carry on commerce and other private business. The final clause declared that all previous quarrels between the two sides would be forgotten, and no claims arising from such quarrels would be entertained. If citizens of one country committed crimes in the other they were to be handed over to their own nation's authorities for execution.[10]

A Soviet encyclopedia issued in 1954 hails the Treaty of Nerchinsk as a "great success of Russian diplomacy," pointing out that it confirmed Russian possession of Eastern Siberia.[11] But subsequent developments were to show that Russia was by no means satisfied with the gains ratified in Nerchinsk. As we shall see, Russia wanted not only the Amur Basin which had been denied it at Nerchinsk but also much beyond. From the Chinese point of view, however, the Nerchinsk Treaty was a victory in that for 170 years it halted Russian imperialism's progress in the Far East. Prince San-go-tu had drawn a line which was to last almost two centuries. Few others who negotiated with Russia in that era could make a comparable claim.

CHAPTER III

From Kyakhta to St. Petersburg

Voyevat Ili Torgovat (Fight or Trade), these were the two alternative Far Eastern policies for Russia which Peter the Great turned over in his mind at the beginning of the eighteenth century. Sometimes he dreamed of extending his dominion to the Great Wall of China itself. But the main line of his policy, and that of his successors until the middle of the nineteenth century, was more cautious. There was sympathy at the Romanov court for the adventurers who time and again suggested a bolder policy against China. But Russia's resources were limited; there were frequent wars and threats of wars on Russia's European frontiers; the Far East was many thousands of miles away from St. Petersburg and Moscow; and the account the Chinese forces had given of themselves in the fighting before Nerchinsk convinced the more sober heads in the Russian capital that the potential gains did not warrant the likely costs of an active aggressive policy. For roughly a century and a half after the Treaty of Nerchinsk, therefore, China was a secondary preoccupation of Russia's. Diplomacy, intrigue and trade were the instruments of Russian policy toward China during this period until it was climaxed at the end of the 1850's by a series of major gains at China's expense. Those gains proved that the expansionist dreams of earlier generations had not been forgotten.

The Treaty of Nerchinsk had defined the extreme eastern section of the Russian-Chinese border, but it had not

solved all problems between the two nations. It left undefined the Russian border with Mongolia, an area in which
there had been Russian-Chinese rivalry during much of
the seventeenth century. Moreover, the Russians were interested in permanent and extensive trade arrangements.
They knew their abundant supply of Siberian furs commanded an active and profitable demand in China. Peter
the Great's advances in stimulating Russian industry substantially widened the list of goods Russia wanted to sell in
China. And from China the Russians wanted silver, precious stones of various kinds and other more mundane but
useful goods, notably tea.

Russia's first diplomatic move after Nerchinsk was to
send a new envoy to Peking, the West European merchant Izbrand Ides. His mission had several objectives: to
set up regular trade arrangements; to find out what Russian goods could be sold in China; to arrange for the return of Russian prisoners of war and refugees living in
China; and to get permission to build a Russian Orthodox
church in Peking, among others. When he got to Peking in
1693, Ides did not find a particularly good atmosphere for
his negotiations. The Chinese rulers were not very interested in trade and they were suspicious of Russia's intentions and maneuvers in Mongolia. The mandarins were
glad, therefore, to utilize a detail which they interpreted
as a slight on the dignity of the Chinese Emperor, the fact
that in the Tsar's letter Ides had brought, the titles of the
Tsar were recited before those of the Emperor. Ides was
humiliated at a public audience and his letter returned to
him. But the envoy persisted and his stay was not without
fruit after almost a year's negotiations. Russian trade caravans were to be permitted to arrive in Peking once every
three years and to stay for 80 days, and Russia could trade
without paying duties on the goods it exported and imported. But Ides could not get permission for a Russian
church to be built in Peking. To his arguments that Russian *émigrés* there needed a church which could also serve
the Russian merchants, the Manchus replied loftily: "It is
impossible that churches for all neighboring and distant

states be established in Peking." Behind this refusal was probably the Chinese fear that such a church would become a center for Russian intrigue and influence in the capital. The Jesuits, who at this time still commanded considerable influence in Peking, also could hardly have been favorable toward establishment of a rival Christian church in a capital whose rulers the Roman Catholic Church hoped to win over.

Peter the Great spurred the trade with China, seeing in it a source of the wealth he needed to finance his wars and his domestic industrialization program. The trade grew swiftly. The first trade expedition sent by his treasury in 1693 carried goods worth 41,900 rubles; by 1710 such expeditions were bringing goods worth 200,000 rubles. Peter was interested in maximizing his treasury's profits. Annoyed by the competition of private traders, he prohibited private commerce in 1706. But private enterprise was not to be stilled so easily; illegal Russian caravans arrived in Peking, apparently often posing as official missions, while the personnel of the treasury caravans continued to make sure that they personally profited from the long and arduous trips.

A growing shadow was cast over this thriving commerce, however, by Chinese suspicions of Russian intentions and activities in Mongolia. The Mongols had split into many rival groups and were very greatly weakened after the heyday of their empire had passed. One of the regional Mongol rulers, the Altyn Khan, had supposedly signed in 1634 a document recognizing he was a subject of the Tsar, and the Chinese feared Russian claims arising from the act of submission. Chinese suzerainty over Mongolia was established during 1688–1696, in part as the result of brilliant military victories by the forces of Emperor Kang-Hsi over the Western Mongol troops led by Prince Galdan who had good relations with Russia.

Chinese suspicions of Russia in Mongolia arose from several factors. One was the growing importance and activity of private Russian merchants in Urga (later Ulan Bator) in Outer, or Northern, Mongolia. A second cause

was the series of attempts by Peter the Great's emissaries
to convert the Mongol spiritual leader in Urga to the Russian Orthodox faith. But the most serious factor around
1720 was the increasing flight of Mongols to Russian territory, flight induced by their unwillingness to supply
Chinese armies in Mongolia with the horses and other
provisions they demanded. The Treaty of Nerchinsk had
provided for the return of such deserters, but the Russians
ignored it, much to Chinese annoyance. As a result of
these suspicions, China made a series of efforts to isolate
Mongolia from Russia. But for full success the Chinese
needed a formal treaty clearly defining the border between Russia and China, and they pressed for one while
the Russians stalled.

The Chinese began showing their displeasure increasingly after 1710. They tightened controls over Mongolia
and sought to prevent contacts between local Mongol
khans and the Russian government. A Russian caravan
that arrived in Peking in 1717 found major difficulties put
in the way of its sales activities, and the next year a Russian caravan was prohibited from passing through Chinese
territory. These and other difficulties induced Peter the
Great to send a new envoy to Peking, Lev Izmailov, who
arrived there in November 1720. His instructions were to
secure the removal of the Chinese restrictions on trade, to
have his secretary, Lorents Langa, accepted as the first
permanent Russian consul in Peking and to reassure the
Chinese that Russian forts being built in Siberia were not
intended for aggression southward. The Manchu Emperor
soon made clear to Izmailov that he was uninterested in
trade but very much interested in getting a final Russian-
Mongolian border treaty and in having the Mongol refugees in Russia returned. Izmailov pleaded he was not empowered to negotiate on these two matters. The result of
the mission was therefore unsatisfactory from the Russian
point of view. Izmailov did not get the new trade treaty
he wanted nor permission to have a permanent Russian
consulate in Peking. Instead, he got oral permission for
Langa to remain in Peking and for a new Russian caravan

to come to that city. But when the caravan arrived in December 1721 its leader found that he was required to sell his best furs to the Manchu court at artificially low prices. General irritation on both sides reached a peak in the spring of 1722. The Chinese had captured several Russians fighting alongside their enemies, the Western Mongols or Dzungars. In retaliation they put a strict guard around Langa's residence, allegedly to protect him. Angered, Langa threatened that when Russia was through with its then current war against Sweden Russian armies would descend upon China. This was too much for the Manchu authorities and they ordered Langa and the caravan personnel out, complaining at the same time of the Russian failure to return the refugees and of the absence of any progress on the boundary issue. About the same time all Russian traders were expelled from Mongolia and all Russian-Chinese trade in Peking halted for several years.

The resolution of these difficulties followed the death of Emperor Kang-Hsi at the end of 1722 and of Peter the Great in early 1725. Kang-Hsi's successor, his son Yung Chen, seems to have decided to improve relations with Russia as a means of strengthening China's position in its continuing wars with the Western Mongols. In July 1724 his emissaries met at a border area near Selenginsk with Langa. They informed him that the Emperor wanted good relations with Russia and was displeased with the ministers who had prohibited Russian trade in Peking and ordered Langa's expulsion. They suggested Langa return to Peking and begin negotiations on a border treaty.

Count Savva Vladislavich Raguzinsky was the man selected by the Russian court to conduct the negotiations. His instructions were to get a trade treaty or other arrangement that would permit resumption of Russian-Chinese trade, to settle the problems of the Mongolian border and the deserters, to get land on which to build a Russian church in Peking and to gather all the intelligence he could on China's resources and strength. Arriving in Peking in October 1726 with a large party of 100 counselors and servants and 1,500 soldiers, he soon showed himself to be an excellent diplomat and intelligence officer. He established good relations with the influential Jesuits and bribed court officials to get secret information. The negotiations begun at Peking and later transferred to the border area were long, difficult and often filled with tension and threats of conflict. Finally two treaties were signed, at Bur (August 21, 1727) and Kyakhta (October 21,1727). The Treaty of Kyakhta, the more important of the two, was a major compromise. The Chinese gave up some territory they had claimed, but in return Russia recognized Chinese sovereignty over Mongolia—a sovereignty Russia was to help destroy almost two centuries later.

The Treaty of Kyakhta defined the border between Russia and China in the area of Mongolia as running from the Sayan Mountains and Sapintabakha on the west to the Argun River in the east. It left the boundary in the Uda River Valley undefined, as it had been in the Treaty of Nerchinsk. Russian trade caravans were to be permitted to visit Peking once every three years, but Russian traders were prohibited from being active in Mongolia. Instead, border trade was to be concentrated at the towns of Nerchinsk and Kyakhta, and was to be under the joint control of authorities representing both countries. Once again, as at Nerchinsk almost four decades earlier, it was agreed that each side should hand back future deserters or criminals who crossed the border from the other side. Russia also received the right to send language students to China and to establish a diplomatic and ecclesiastical mission in Peking.

Count Raguzinsky feared that the authorities in Russia's capital would be displeased with the treaty. He had several of his assistants at the negotiations and several Mongol chiefs sign a statement declaring "the newly established frontier is highly advantageous to Russia and . . . Russian possessions have been extended into Mongolia a distance of several days' march and in certain sections of even several weeks."[1] But this defense proved inadequate, and in 1731 he had to answer his critics at home in other terms.

At Kyakhta, he declared, he had had the alternative of accepting the treaty or seeing war between Russia and China. Then he stated the case against war in these terms:

> We may conceive of a war with China, but we must take into consideration that this would not be an easy undertaking. We would have to concentrate at the border at least ten regiments of the line and an equal number of regiments of irregulars, which would have to face all the Chinese forces and perhaps the Mongolian as well. The cost of such an undertaking, even assuming that it should be successful, will never be recovered, even in a hundred years. We would have to build fortresses, maintain strong garrisons there, supply them continuously with food and ammunition. Peace would be menaced for a long time, trade with China would be interrupted, and the Siberian population would become impoverished. Moreover, the Chinese would never acknowledge defeat, they would begin to arm themselves to an even greater extent and learn our military arts.[2]

But other opinions were being pressed in St. Petersburg, too. Thus in 1733, on his way home from Peking, Langa made this evaluation:

> At this moment the Chinese are in a critical position. Engaged in a terrible fight with the Dzungars, they are afraid of Russia and at the same time look to us to supply their armies with provisions and horses. The moment is most opportune to intervene in Peking and demand that all restrictions imposed upon our caravans be removed; that the Russian mission be freed of the insufferable surveillance of the Mandarins which hinders all trade; and that the dispute concerning frontiers be settled favorably. As long as the Dzungars keep the Chinese in check on the battlefields, the latter will not dare defy the Russian Court. We even believe that this is an excellent time to seek the extension of our frontier to the Amur River.[3]

A few words should be said at this point about the difference in position relative to China between Russia

and the other European powers. The Russians first came
into overland contact with China, as we have seen. The
basic problem in their relations during the late seventeenth
and early eighteenth centuries was the definition of the
frontier between the two countries. In the complex process of infiltration, fighting and negotiation that preceded
the Nerchinsk and Kyakhta determinations, China was finally forced by the facts of geography and power to deal
with Russia as an effective equal. The other European
powers, however, were in a far more disadvantageous
position in this initial stage of China's relations with the
modern West. The English, the Dutch and the Portuguese
came by sea in small numbers and weak force. The
Dutch, it is true, conquered Formosa in 1642, but they
lost it twenty years later to the forces of the Chinese pi-
rate Koxinga. The basic pattern in these early years of
western penetration was set in the ghetto-like enclaves at
Macao (established by the Portuguese in 1557) and then at
Canton where the British established a permanent building
for trade in 1715, in the period between the Treaties of
Nerchinsk and Kyakhta. What Canton was for the British
and other Europeans, therefore, the town of Kyakhta was
for the Russians, but in addition the Russians had the right
to send caravans directly into Peking, though that, true
enough, only once every three years. Early in the eighteenth century Peter the Great suggested that Russia, too,
should establish maritime trade with China through Canton
as a supplement to its long overland route, but that was
not to happen until the nineteenth century.

The first Chinese diplomatic mission to Russia arrived in
Moscow on January 14, 1731. It was greeted with an artillery salute of 31 rounds and by massed regiments and
orchestras designed to show the majesty and might of the
Russian state. The purpose of this mission was primarily
to ask for Russian neutrality in the renewed Chinese warfare with the Western Mongols. The envoys told the Moscow authorities that they should not be suspicious of
Chinese troop movements near the Russian border. They

asked for permission to visit the khans of the Volga Kalmyks, subjects of Russia, hoping to enlist the support of the latter in the war against the Western Mongols. The Chinese also requested the Russians not to provide refuge in Russia for the Mongol troops and to imprison under guard any such troops that did get across the border. The Russians for their part thanked the envoys for the information on the troop movements. They permitted the visit to the Kalmyks, but warned that this was an exception and in the future the Chinese would have to make such contacts through the Russian envoy in Peking. For their part, the Russians complained about violations of the trade provision of the Kyakhta Treaty, charging that a treasury caravan which had arrived in Peking in 1727 had had to return home with part of its goods unsold. In 1732 another Chinese mission arrived in Russia. While it was in Moscow, the Russians showed its members factories and cultural places of interest. These were the first two Chinese embassies to foreign countries.

But matters did not improve for the Russian caravans. Government agents met strong competition in Peking from private Russian traders there. Moreover, Manchu officials put many obstacles in the way of sales. They demanded bribes and tried to have the Russian goods sold at low prices. Efforts to replace the government caravans with trade by a private company failed because Russian merchants found it more profitable to operate in company with an official caravan and—with the connivance of Tsarist officials—to shift any losses they suffered onto the government account. In 1756 the passage of the caravans was finally ended, though long before that the volume of goods brought by each caravan had fallen well below the peaks of 1711–1717. As a result, the border town of Kyakhta became essentially the main center of Russian-Chinese trade, a status it enjoyed well into the nineteenth century.

There was a good deal of friction between Russia and China in the Mongolian border area during the middle and late eighteenth century. At times this friction arose from trade disputes over tariffs, smuggling activities, incursions of tribesmen from Russia into China and the like. These factors led to the closing of the Kyakhta market at Chinese insistence several times, during 1764–1768, 1779 and 1785–1792. Nevertheless trade at Kyakhta grew rapidly from the 1750's to 1800.

Potentially more serious were the complications of the Chinese clashes with their subject peoples. The Chinese were furious when the Russians gave refuge in the middle of the eighteenth century to the Western Mongol leader Amursana, and Chinese forces violated the Russian border in pursuit of this Dzungar chief. In 1756 Outer Mongolia revolted against Chinese rule, and five leading Mongol chiefs approached the Russian commander of Selenginsk, Jacobi, asking him to arrange with the Russian court to accept Mongolia as a protectorate and its people as Russian subjects. This request came at a critical time, when the main Chinese forces were far away in the west; Jacobi's superior, Governor Myatlev, pointed out to St. Petersburg that acceptance of the proposal would mean that "the Chinese force will be cut off from its base, and Russia will be able to dictate terms to Peking." But by the time St. Petersburg had made up its mind on this delicate issue, the revolt had been suppressed and the opportunity was gone. Great indeed was the bitterness of the Mongols, the Russians in Siberia and their friends at the court who looked with greedy eyes at the Chinese empire to the south. When the Russian Senate sought to gain concessions from China for its neutrality in the fighting, the Chinese sneered back that Russia had failed to intervene only because it did not have the strength to do so. If Russia had intervened, the Chinese continued, the Russian troops would have been defeated as completely as the Western Mongols. The Russians snapped back that their country occupied almost half the world and was not to be treated like the primitive Mongols or the small Tartar tribes. The Chinese replied that it was ridiculous to compare any sovereign with China's omnipotent Emperor, especially if the sovereign were a mere female—the latter gibe was directed, of course, at the then ruler of Russia, Catherine the Great. This exchange, it is worth mentioning, took place when Russian troops had defeated Frederick the Great and entered Berlin. But Mongolia and China proper were much further from St. Petersburg than Berlin. Hence the Russian court kept its temper and there was no war, though advocates of such a war as the means of enlarging Russia's domain were not absent from Catherine's entourage.

If some Russians dreamed of expansion at China's expense, the Chinese wanted only to be left alone and to have as little as possible to do with the Russians. Peking's policy, therefore, sought to create a wide expanse of thinly populated buffer areas along the full length of the Russian-Chinese border. Some peoples living near the border were evacuated; in the Amur River area, settlement of Chinese and Manchus was forbidden. Chinese emigration into Mongolia was largely barred during the nineteenth century, leaving that vast area the preserve of the relatively small number of Mongols. Between 1750 and 1850, the Manchu Emperors sought also to hinder Chinese migration into central and northern Manchuria, hoping thus to save their patrimony from Sinification. The effort was not entirely successful, but it was effective enough so that in the middle of the nineteenth century the Manchurian part of the border with Russia was still thinly populated.

Trade between China and Russia boomed at Kyakhta during this period. In 1769 the total value of this commerce was about 2,000,000 rubles; by 1781 it was valued at almost 7,500,000 rubles. It declined somewhat after that but then recovered again to reach a new peak of more than 13,000,000 rubles in 1810. The trade volume plunged more than 50 per cent in 1812, reflecting the impact of Napoleon's invasion of Russia, but by 1826 the commerce was back up to more than 12,000,000 rubles. However, in the early nineteenth century Kyakhta's future became more and more clouded as Western Europe's seaborne trade with China grew steadily. Merchants in Central and Western Europe no longer found it attractive to send their goods to China over the long land route to Kyakhta; it was far cheaper to send them by sea to Canton. Conversely, buyers in European Russia began to find it cheaper to buy Chinese goods coming by sea to Europe's Atlantic, Baltic and Mediterranean ports. And finally a new land route for Russian trade with China began to open up, this time in Central Asia where Russia met China in Sinkiang.

In its heyday, during the century after 1750, the trade at Kyakhta normally involved annually goods worth millions of dollars at current prices. It was a barter trade in which commodities were exchanged against commodities and sale for money was prohibited. The participants were private merchants, combined on the Russian side in various special companies authorized by the Tsar, and on the Chinese side into highly organized groups. The tight organization and strict discipline among the Chinese merchants excited the Russians' admiration, convincing them often that the Chinese had all the advantages in bargaining and made the more advantageous deals. A Russian account declares that each evening the Chinese official in charge of this trade convened the Chinese merchants in a meeting which decided what goods would be offered the next day in Kyakhta and what prices would be charged. Each Chinese merchant would be assigned certain goods for his participation in this trade. Any violation of the decisions regarding prices and goods was punished by penalties of varying severity. An offender could be barred from trading for periods of six days to two months, or he could be banished altogether from Maimachen, the Chinese border town where the merchants lived. When deemed necessary, corporal punishment of up to 50 blows with a bamboo cane was administered to offenders. On the Russian side, efforts were made to achieve similar organization. The Russian companies selected representatives who met to establish their own valuations for the goods being bought and sold. Before 1800 the value of all goods was set in units of Chinese cotton cloth, the so-called *kitaika;* beginning in 1800 the unit of common value was a given weight of Chinese tea. But all efforts on both sides to organize matters did not prevent disputes and hard feelings and, on the part of the Russians at least, the feeling that they were being out-traded.

The substantial growth of Kyakhta trade during the first decades of the nineteenth century was partly the result of the growing popularity of tea-drinking in Russia. Between the first and third decades of the century Russian purchases of tea at Kyakhta almost doubled. In 1825 tea purchases accounted for 87.3 per cent of all Chinese goods bought there. On the Russian side furs, and for a time cloth and textile products played the leading role. Many of the goods the Russians sold at Kyakhta came from Western Europe; Silesian cloth from Prussia was particularly important. But this trade in cloth declined after 1820 because of the competition of British cloth coming into China through Canton.

In 1800 the Russian government stepped in to regulate the trade at Kyakhta. The Russian traders were prohibited from changing the prices they bought and sold goods for. If demand conditions changed or traders wanted to get rid of goods they had held for an excessive time, merchants had to petition government officials for a changed price. The decision on such an appeal had to be made by the entire company of traders in formal session either the same day the petition was handed in, or the very next day. A merchant who sold Russian goods for less than the established price or bought Chinese goods at a price above the established quotation was fined 15 per cent of the value of the goods involved. If he repeated the offense, he was expelled from Kyakhta and forbidden to engage in the trade. Any Russian merchant who attempted to use gold, silver or opium in his trade or traded for money had the goods or money confiscated and was expelled from that area of Siberia altogether. The proclaimed purpose of these regulations was to minimize the number of Russian-Chinese trade quarrels, but clearly the Russian government was also anxious to exercise as near a monopoly control over the prices in this trade as it could, and thus to duplicate what was believed to be the Chinese control. On the Chinese side, too, merchants were warned against acting out of individual greed and instructed that the advantage of the individual trader must play a secondary role to the common advantage.

Early in the nineteenth century, the Russians finally made efforts to begin a sea trade with China. The motives were in part economic. It was one-third to one-half cheaper to move tea by sea from China to England than to transport it overland from Kyakhta to Moscow, and the sea voyage took only half or a third as long a time. Adding to the economic pressure was the growth of the Russian fur catch in Alaska, Kamchatka, Sakhalin and other Russian areas in the North Pacific. It was clearly much more convenient and cheaper to move these furs to China by boat than to deliver them to the relatively inaccessible trade center at Kyakhta. Finally Russian interest in a sea route to the Pacific grew after the appearance of French and British naval expeditions in the North Pacific in the 1780's and 1790's. These expeditions aroused apprehensions about the future of Russian holdings in this area, and the search began for a way to supply and man these distant possessions by sea as an alternative to the long, slow and expensive land route across Siberia.

As a result, the Russian-American Company in 1803 sent out two ships, the *Nadezhda* and the *Neva,* to investigate sea routes to the Pacific and Indian Oceans. They were to bring food and other supplies to the Russian settlements on the American continent and then take furs from these settlements to Canton. The ships accomplished their mission, arriving in Canton with their furs in December 1805. While they were trading, word came from Peking that Russians were forbidden to trade by sea since they already had land privileges, and Russian ships were ordered to leave immediately. A diplomatic effort to arrange for Russian ships to use Canton failed in 1805 when a mission headed by Count Y. A. Golovkin set out for Peking and got no further than the city of Urga, where it was refused permission to proceed and turned back. This first effort to trade by sea was not followed up significantly for the next half century.

In the 1840's the attention of Russian imperialists turned once again to the possibility of new territorial gains at the expense of China. One reason was China's glaring weakness so vividly exposed during the Opium War which Britain won at the beginning of the decade. A second reason was the fear that if Russia did not move to strenghten her position *vis-à-vis* China and make such gains as she could, the British would become dominant in China and would seize territories that might otherwise go to Russia. And if that happened, might not Britain and other Western powers move also against existing Russian possessions in the North Pacific? The powerful combination of opportunity, greed and fear was at work in a Russia still basking in the dimming glory of its successful defense against Napoleon. There were important and influential figures at the court in St. Petersburg, notably the chancellor, Count Nesselrode, who looked askance at the idea of adventure so far away. They could see little worthwhile gain and much grief from the enmity of China and Britain that might result. But these more cautious souls were overruled by the chief imperialist, Tsar Nicholas I.

The man Nicholas selected for the task of achieving territorial gains in the Far East was the governor of Tula Province in European Russia, the young (38), energetic, able and ambitious Nikolai Muraviev. At seven o'clock of a September morning in 1847, at a railroad station near Tula, the Tsar informed Muraviev he had been appointed governor general of Eastern Siberia. The Tsar emphasized to his appointee how vast this domain was—stretching from the Yenisei River to the Bering Strait—saying: "If any power seizes Kamchatka, you in Irkutsk will only find out about it six months later." During conversation with Muraviev, the Tsar—after touching on relations with China—said: "As for the Russian river Amur, you will

hear from us later." The Tsar ended his talk with the re-
mark: "To one who knows how to listen, even a few
words are enough to understand." A far stupider man than
Muraviev would have known what was meant.

It is a sign of Soviet embarrassment over Muraviev's
accomplishments that his biography in a recent (1959)
encyclopedia is summed up in 40 words. Actually this mid-
nineteenth century Russian empire builder is one of the
most interesting characters in the whole long history of
Russian-Chinese relations. A loyal and effective servant of
the Tsar, he yet had advanced and even radical ideas for
his time. In the 1850's he opposed serfdom, struck up
personal friendships with anarchists, did what he could to
ease the lot of Siberian political prisoners and dreamed
of a Russian-American alliance that would dominate the
North Pacific. Mikhail Bakunin, the founder of modern
anarchism, wrote in 1860: "Muraviev is the only man
among all those who have power and influence in Russia
who can and must fully and without the least reservation
be considered one of us."[4] Yet this same Muraviev was a
fanatical Russian expansionist, a man capable of every
kind of deception to accomplish his goals. In retrospect it
seems clear that, in his combination of radical political
views and Russian expansionism, Muraviev was an early
example of a human type the world has become familiar
with more than once since the Bolshevik Revolution.

In his confidential memoranda to his superiors, Muraviev made no secret of his ambitions and plans. He wrote
the Tsar in 1853: "There can be no doubt that . . . we
must gain control of Sakhalin and the estuary of the Amur
River." While China reeled under the blows of her foes,
he mused in a memorandum: "If the defeat of China
should entail the fall of her dynasty, this outcome would
of course be most favorable to Russia. . . . Our neigh-
bors, Manchuria and Mongolia, would become (in fact, if
not in name) our possessions, and Russia would finally acquire all that she could here desire."[5]

Writing to the Grand Duke Constantine, Muraviev expressed both his fears and his hopes as he surveyed the

world scene. Some of his musings have a contemporary ring if due account is taken of altered circumstances:

While the Western powers could not inflict any serious loss on Russia in Europe, they might easily deprive her of Kamchatka and of the mouth of the Amur in the Far East. The empire of China, now insignificant on account of its military weakness, might become dangerous under the influence and guidance of England and France—Siberia might even cease to be Russian. The loss of this vast region . . . could not be compensated by any victories or conquests in the West. It was therefore necessary to guard Kamchatka, Sakhalin, and the mouth of the Amur, thus also acquiring enduring influence on China.[6]

Muraviev's tactics were simplicity itself and won a vast area with virtually no fighting. He built up Russian forces in the Far East, intruded upon the Amur Valley, set up fortified posts and settlements along the river's banks and presented the Chinese with a *fait accompli* which the Chinese had to accept. In accomplishing all this Muraviev had valuable aid from Captain, later Admiral, Gennadi Nevelskoy, commander of the Russian naval force in the Far East during the 1850's. It was Nevelskoy who struck the first direct blow at Chinese dominion of the area, sailing up the Amur in 1850 and establishing a post he named Nikolayevsk in honor of the Tsar. The intrusion on Chinese sovereignty, enthusiastically backed by Muraviev, provoked heated debate in St. Petersburg. The debate was resolved by the Tsar's famous words: "Where the Russian flag has once been hoisted, it must not be lowered." The die was cast.

In the early 1850's Muraviev built up his military forces in the Far East, while Nevelskoy continued his exploration of the Amur and discovered that Sakhalin was an island, not a peninsula as had been thought. In the spring of 1854 Muraviev directed a large fleet of barges, rafts, and one steamer down the Amur, a fleet carrying more than 1,000 soldiers and their artillery. The local Chinese officials were appalled but overawed by this power and did nothing to stop this flagrant violation of the Treaty of Nerchinsk. The next year Muraviev led an even larger and more powerful fleet down the Amur, this time bringing along more than 8,000 persons as well as cattle to help set up permanent settlements. In 1856 a third expedition bringing still more soldiers, settlers and supplies for the new settlements on the Amur went down the river. This had now really become a Russian river, a fact recognized by the Tsar's *ukaz* of October 31, 1856 which set up a new administrative region, the Maritime Province, including the Amur territory, Kamchatka and the Okhotsk coast. In 1867 Muraviev sent a fourth expedition down the river, bringing more Cossack infantry plus cavalry troops. Russia had lost the Crimean War far to the west during the time these expeditions had seized a new region, but these Far Eastern gains were at least a partial compensation.

Occupied with war against France and England and struggle against the Taiping rebels, the Peking government could do little except protest. Finally it sent Prince I Shan to negotiate with Muraviev at the Chinese town of Aigun. In 1689, at Nerchinsk, the Chinese had been able to impose their will upon the Russians because they had had the preponderance of military force. Now the shoe was on the other foot. Muraviev made plain his intention of having Russian ownership of the area north of the Amur, regardless of what the Treaty of Nerchinsk said. Behind his words was a well armed force of more than 20,000 men, while the Chinese troops in the area were relatively few in number and very poorly equipped. Moreover, there was a Russian fleet near Aigun and Muraviev used the threat that it might act as an effective bargaining counter. On May 28, 1858, the Treaty of Aigun was finally signed. In this treaty China ceded to Russia the left bank of the Amur River down to the Ussuri, while the area between the Ussuri and the Pacific Ocean was to belong in common to the two nations until the issues here were decided at a future date. Some 185,000 square miles had been won by Russia. It is characteristic of much of

Russian policy in China in the nineteenth and early twentieth centuries that this act of imperialism was presented to the Chinese as an expression of Russian anxiety to "protect" China against a supposed threat from England. What the Chinese thought of the treaty was indicated by Peking's angry reaction. I Shan was dismissed and denounced "for stupidity and overstepping his authority."

In June 1858, the month following the Treaty of Aigun, another Russian-Chinese treaty was signed in Tientsin. The Russian negotiator here was Admiral Evfimi Putyatin, whose negotiating authority was confined to commercial matters. By this treaty Russia was granted commercial rights in China similar to those enjoyed by England and other Western powers. It could trade with China by sea as well as overland, and its ships could use Shanghai, Canton, Amoy, Ningpo and other open ports available to the Western powers. The treaty provided for a regular monthly courier service between Kyakhta and Peking, confirmed Russia's right to send envoys to Peking and permitted Russian consuls to reside in the open ports. These consuls, like their Western European counterparts, were given extraterritorial jurisdiction over Russian citizens violating Chinese laws.

But Putyatin's treaty, negotiated and signed before he knew of the gains at Aigun, had not solved the territorial problem. The Aigun Treaty was not ratified and instead the Chinese threatened to halt trade with Russia at Kyakhta and in Sinkiang. Chinese sources put out word that Aigun had been only an expression of the Emperor's "good will toward the poor Russian settlers, and his willingness to allow them to reside in some places of the Amur Basin and to cultivate the lands that were not occupied by anybody else." The negotiations on these matters carried out by a new Russian envoy, General Nikolai Ignatiev, became so heated that he left Peking in May 1860, effectively breaking off diplomatic negotiations.

Here history played into Russia's hands. The Chinese government was weak and in disorder under the cumulative blows of the British and the French on the one hand,

and of the Taiping rebels on the other. At Tientsin in 1858 Putyatin's treaty had been one of four similar treaties the Chinese had signed with Russia, Britain, France, and the United States. But they had signed only after being subjected to extreme Western diplomatic and military pressure. Ignatiev had had no difficulty in 1859 in exchanging ratification documents for the Treaty of Tientsin with the Chinese, but the British and French ran into what they considered provocative delays in getting their treaties finally ratified. As a result, fighting broke out between the Chinese and the Anglo-French forces. This fighting culminated in the Western capture of Tientsin and Peking in the late summer and early fall of 1860. The looting and destruction of the beautiful Summer Palace of the Emperor in Peking by the victors shocked the Chinese but they were helpless.

At this point General Ignatiev, now back in Peking, re-entered the picture and accomplished one of the most skillful feats of diplomatic double-dealing in history. Some such possibility appears to have been envisaged in St. Petersburg when he was first given his assignment in 1859. Admiral Putyatin had suggested that Russia try to gain advantages from China's military weakness *vis-à-vis* the British and French by offering military aid to the Peking government. Hence Ignatiev brought experts in various military fields with him. His instructions called for him to try to mediate between the Western powers and the Chinese, and in particular to try to prevent the Manchu dynasty—with which all Russian-Chinese treaties had been signed—from collapsing. But if the Manchus did fall from power, he was to try to keep Manchuria, Mongolia and the Kashgar area in northwest China for Russia.

When the Anglo-French allies reached the Peking area, Ignatiev showed the British commander a detailed map of the city and recommended the capital's north gate as the weakest spot in its defenses. The British commander later testified that the map was of "great value." Almost simultaneously Ignatiev offered his services as mediator to the Peking government. As the price for his services he demanded not only ratification of the Treaty of Aigun but also extension of the Russian-Chinese boundary line along the Ussuri River to the limits of Korea and the establishment of Russian consulates in several cities. The Chinese accepted his proposition. In the days that followed, Ignatiev was the "never-failing counselor" to the British general as well as the mediator expecting rich rewards from the Chinese. After the latter had conceded to the British the desired principle of Western diplomatic residence in Peking, Ignatiev persuaded the British general that Peking was unsafe in winter and that he should leave as soon as possible. Once the allied troops had left, Ignatiev was free to deal with the Chinese, who paid his price by accepting the Treaty of Peking, signed on November 14, 1860.[7]

The Treaty of Peking brought the Russians major territorial and other gains. Its first article completed the work begun in Aigun two years earlier by making Russian the whole area between the Ussuri River and the Pacific Ocean, adding an additional 133,000 square miles to Russian territory. The boundaries of Russia were thus brought to the frontier of Korea, and the earlier Russian founding of the city of Vladivostok (Rule of the East) at a magnificent harbor on the Pacific in this region was retroactively legalized. An even larger territorial gain was made in Central Asia. There the Chinese surrendered their claim to almost 350,000 square miles of territory by agreeing that the boundary between Sinkiang and Russian Central Asia be set along the line of permanent pasture markers, or pickets, the Chinese had set up to limit pasture use by the Kazakh nomads. Later the Chinese tried in vain to have the border follow the temporary pasture pickets which really marked the limits of Chinese territorial claims, but by then it was too late. The Treaty of Tarbagatai in 1864 finally delimited the boundary in this area on the principles agreed to at Peking.

The non-territorial gains were also significant. Russian merchants were given the right to travel for trade purposes from Kyakhta to Peking, trading en route in the cities of Urga and Kalgan. Russia was permitted to maintain a consulate in Urga. In Sinkiang, where an earlier agreement had allowed Russian-Chinese trade at Kuldja and Tarbagatai, trade was permitted also at Kashgar and Russian consulates were permitted to function in all three of these cities. Citizens of each country, the treaty provided, were to be allowed in the other and "in places open for trade can carry on commercial activities completely freely, without any limitations from local authorities; they can also freely visit at any time markets, shops, or homes of local merchants, sell and buy different goods at wholesale or retail, for money or by means of barter, and borrow or lend on the basis of mutual trust." Russian extraterritorial rights over Russian citizens in China were confirmed.

The Russian territorial gains at China's expense which were won by the Treaties of Aigun and Peking were, of course, typical examples of imperialist encroachment on a weak Asian power. At the time, the duplicity employed by the Tsar's representatives was not considered particularly extraordinary, and it was taken for granted that the strong took advantage of the weak. But now, slightly more than a century later, both the world balances of forces and generally accepted standards of international morality have changed. In early 1963 the Chinese government publicly called into question the validity of the gains made by the Tsar in 1858 and 1860, gains remaining under Soviet rule. Soviet historians appear to have anticipated such a challenge. In the *Diplomatichesky Slovar* (Diplomatic Dictionary) issued in 1960, Soviet historians asserted that the Aigun Treaty "returned to Russia the territory given to China by the Treaty of Nerchinsk." And as though preparing for a Chinese attack on the Aigun settlement, they gave this account to rationalize and justify the territorial gains made:

In 1861 the Russian government informed the Chinese imperial government that, guarding the mouth of the Amur and Sakhalin from occupation by other powers and taking account of the fact that in this area no border had been established, it had taken measures to erect fortifications. The appearance of the British fleet off the Kamchatka coast during the Crimean War forced the Russian government to hasten the solution of the Amur problem. Muraviev, who was charged with the negotiations, convinced the Chinese representatives of the necessity of demarcation at the Amur, citing the danger both for Russia and for China of English penetration into the lower Amur and the difficulty of defending this region which lacked roads and had no communications along the Amur. Not seeing any advantage from having the left bank of the Amur and understanding that it could not defend the Amur region against English encroachment with its own forces, the Peking government reached agreement with Russia.[8]

The facts, as we have seen, were more complicated and less flattering to Russia's straightforwardness than this account.

We have seen that by a series of treaties—Nerchinsk, Kyakhta, Aigun and Peking—the Russian-Chinese border was defined from the western end of Mongolia to the Pacific Ocean. But a new major border between the two countries came into being in the nineteenth century, in Central Asia. That border, not finally fixed until near the end of the century, today divides Soviet Central Asia from Sinkiang. Located in the heart of Asia, the territory involved was the country of the Western Mongols in the eighteenth century and the scene of their frequent wars with the Chinese. In the second half of the nineteenth century this was a land of Moslem peoples—Kalmyks, Uzbeks, Kirghiz and others. The contest between Russia and China here was part of a greater struggle, for Britain then looked askance at the Russian advance in this region, fearing Russian aggression against India. The Russians in turn suspected British schemes to use the Moslem peoples of Sinkiang to displace the newly won Russian power over the similar Moslem peoples of Russian Central Asia. This larger struggle thus pitted Russians against British over a vast region from Persia to China, but we shall focus upon the Russian-Chinese aspects of the matter.

Russian interest in this area began as early as the late eighteenth century, when Russian traders penetrated into western China from Siberia and began trading at Kuldja and Tarbagatai. A Russian, Putimisev, reconnoitered the area in 1811 and reported that Russian textiles and leather were being exchanged at Kuldja for Chinese silver and for Chinese supplies needed by a Russian garrison on the Irtysh River in Siberia. Later Russian trade caravans came from Semipalatinsk and Petropavlovsk, leaving in July or August of one year, taking 50 to 60 days for their journey, and returning to Siberia in March of the following year. Chinese caravans in turn took the Russian goods to Peking through Urumchi and Lanchow. The trade in these cities was small compared to that at Kyakhta, but it grew sharply around 1850. Theoretically this was a barter trade, as at Kyakhta, but by 1851 the Russians were buying almost three times as much as they sold, paying for the deficit in silver or gold and receiving credit from Chinese merchants whose chief sales item was tea. By 1851 tea made up more than 90 per cent of Chinese sales to Russians in western China; the amount of tea sold here had grown very rapidly in the preceding decade. The Russians had no legal protection in this trade until 1851 and grumbled at the restrictions placed upon them by the Manchus. At Kuldja, for example, the Russian caravans had to stop outside the city at a special camp called Small Kuldja and often had to wait several months for word to arrive from Peking permitting them to trade. In 1851, however, a trade treaty was finally agreed on which legalized this trade and put the Russian merchants under the supervision of Russian consuls in both Kuldja and Tarbagatai. In 1860 as we noted above, a third major trading center in western China, the southern city of Kashgar, was opened to Russian trade by the Treaty of Peking.

Meanwhile, during the first half of the nineteenth century there was increasing Russian interest in and penetration of what is now Soviet Central Asia. In this vast desert area with its extremes of climate in summer and winter, the Russian advance was not easy despite the military weakness of such small medieval states as Khiva, Bokhara and Khokand. After some setbacks in earlier decades, the decisive Russian push came in the 1860's. The American Civil War played a part in this timing, since the difficulties of getting American cotton for Russian textile factories made influential industrial circles anxious to get control of the potential cotton-growing areas in Central Asia. By 1870, after the capture of Samarkand and Tashkent, much of Central Asia was under effective Russian control. The increasing Russian presence and strength in Central Asia provided the base from which pressure could be exerted for further expansion to the east at China's expense in Sinkiang.

We have discussed above the delimitation of the border between Sinkiang and Russian Central Asia by the Treaties of Peking (1860) and of Tarbagatai (1864) with the large Chinese territorial losses implied by the decision to follow the line of permanent pasture pickets. But in addition to these gains, the Russians also wanted control of the Ili Valley, a region which had been one of the great routes for trade and invasion in Asia for centuries. In 1857 General Gasfort, the Russian governor general of Western Siberia had declared: "The transformation of Kashgar into a state independent of China under a Russian protectorate would render a great service to its people, for whom the Sino-Manchurian tyranny has become insupportable. . . . We shall make ourselves masters of Central Asia, and we shall be able to hold all the Khans in respect, which will facilitate our march forward."[9]

A Moslem revolt in Sinkiang in 1864 finally gave the Russians their opportunity to penetrate the Ili Valley, though its first effect was to induce the Chinese negotiators to accept the Treaty of Tarbagatai. The Manchu rule over these Moslem peoples was very severe and there had been numerous unsuccessful revolts earlier in the century. This

1864 uprising soon came under the leadership of a talented adventurer of humble origin, a former dancing boy, Yakub Beg. By 1869 Yakub Beg's "Emirate of Djety-shaar" embraced almost all of Sinkiang; the Manchu forces controlled only a thin northern strip of the area. Emboldened by these successes, Yakub Beg dreamed of creating a vast new Moslem empire in the heart of Asia, an empire which would embrace not only Sinkiang but also much or all of Russian Central Asia. To the British, worried about a possible continued Russian push south toward India, the appearance of Yakub Beg's new realm suggested interesting possibilities of a union between Britain and Islam to create a strong buffer area shielding India from the Russians. The latter had little love for Yakub Beg. He had fought against them in Central Asia before coming to Sinkiang. They recognized the explosive possibilities his continued success might have among the Moslems subject to the Tsar. Moreover, the Russians saw no point in offending the Manchu emperors, who had proved so pliable in earlier years, by trying any major intrigues with Yakub Beg. Peking intended to reconquer Sinkiang and needed only time to regain its strength after the debilitating wars with the Western powers and the exhausting struggle against the Taiping rebellion. But events showed that it had also occurred to the Russians that Yakub Beg might be exploited to get more Chinese territory.

The opportunity came in 1871 when Yakub Beg's forces appeared to threaten Kuldja. Instead, Russian troops took the city and a substantial area in the vicinity. The Russian governor general of Turkestan, Kauffman, informed St. Petersburg he had done so to keep British influence out of the region. The Russian foreign office sought to allay alarm in Peking by assuring the authorities there that its forces had merely moved in to restore order and would return the area when Chinese forces were strong enough to return and take over full control. Understandably, many historians suspect St. Petersburg said this blandly, considering it unlikely that Peking's forces in this distant region would ever become strong enough to require fulfillment of this promise. Certainly when the Chinese began negotiations for the region's return in 1872 the Russians had no difficulty in finding reasons for delaying their withdrawal indefinitely. In that same year, too, the Russians made a trade agreement with Yakub Beg opening up his territory for the first time to Tsarist merchants.

In the early 1870's Yakub Beg attempted a complex balancing act. He sought support from the British and accepted arms and a title from the Sultan of Turkey, a move suggesting he was making Sinkiang a vassal state of Russia's bitter enemy on the Bosporus. In 1874 and 1875 Russian troops were therefore concentrated for a possible attack against Kashgar in southern Sinkiang and in 1876 the Russians demanded and got from Yakub Beg strategic mountain passes to the west of Kashgar. At the same time, however, the Russians moved to help the Chinese forces mobilizing against Yakub Beg under the famous general Tso Tung-tang, supplying Tso with necessary grain. In 1876 and 1877 Tso's forces moved quickly and effectively. By the end of 1877 Yakub Beg was dead—a suicide or poisoned, the facts are unclear—and all of Sinkiang was under Chinese control except for the Russian-held enclave around Kuldja. Two Mohammedan leaders who had tried to preserve fragments of Yakub Beg's domain fled into Russia and their repatriation was denied the Chinese on the ground that they were political refugees.

The Chinese began pressing in 1878 for Russian withdrawal from Kuldja and finally after some delays negotiations were opened in St. Petersburg. The Chinese envoy, Chung How, had had some prior international experience but was completely incapable of driving a hard bargain with the Russians. This was proved in the summer of 1879 when he signed the very disadvantageous draft Treaty of Livadia. In this treaty the Russians agreed to vacate the Kuldja area in return for the following: the Tekes Valley—a large, rich territory in the southwestern portion of the occupied area—and passes through the mountains; permission for Russian merchants to be exempt from all duties in trading in Mongolia and Sinkiang; Chinese consent to the opening of Russian consulates in seven additional Sinkiang cities; and payment by China to Russia of 5,000,000 rubles to defray Russian occupation costs.

China was shocked when the terms agreed to at Livadia became known. Not only did Peking repudiate the agreement but it recalled its envoy, imprisoned him and sentenced him to decapitation. He was saved only by appeals for mercy from Queen Victoria and other European notables. An important and influential war party sprang up in Peking demanding that China stand firm at any cost. The redoubtable Tso Tung-tang himself memorialized the Emperor with these words:

> It seems that Russia intends to make Ili (Kuldja) a Russian colony. . . . When a country is defeated in war it may be obliged to cede territory and to sue for peace. Why should China sacrifice an important area to satisfy Russia's greed? It would be like throwing a bone to a dog to prevent it from biting. But when the bone has been eaten up, the dog would still want to bite. The loss at present is apparent and the trouble in the future will be endless.[10]

The eccentric British general Charles G. Gordon entered the scene in the spring of 1880. He had a good reputation in China for his services to the Emperor in helping put down the Taiping Rebellion. His advice to the Chinese government was that it avoid war against Russia at all cost. To do this, he urged, it should agree to pay an indemnity. If war came, he predicted, the Russians would be able to occupy Peking in two months and China's only chance of success would come if it were willing to undergo long years of guerrilla warfare. The Russian actions in massing a large army near Kuldja and assembling a large fleet in the Pacific helped convince the Chinese that negotiation was wiser than war in this situation.

The result was that Tseng Chi-tse, the Chinese minister in Britain, was sent to St. Petersburg to renew negotiations. Accompanied by a Briton and a Frenchman, Tseng found upon his arrival that the Russians were arrogant and inclined to try to get the Treaty of Livadia accepted after all. But Tseng was persistent, conciliatory and firm on essentials. Moreover, the Russians had a healthy respect for Tso's troops and their capabilities if turned against relatively empty Siberia. The result of negotiations finally was the Treaty of St. Petersburg signed in 1881. This treaty was considered by the Chinese at the time as a victory of sorts, since Russia agreed to give up most of the Tekes Valley and the mountain passes, and to keep only a small area west of the Holkutz River. The number of new Russian consulates was reduced, as was the area in which Russian merchants were to enjoy free trade. Against this the Russians secured an increase in the Chinese indemnity payment from the 5,000,000 rubles of Livadia to 9,000,000 rubles.

Thus Chinese sovereignty in Sinkiang was restored and the border with Russia finally demarcated without the major losses that had taken place elsewhere. For several decades thereafter, Sinkiang was relatively quiet in Russia-Chinese relations. In part this was because Russia found more promising possibilities for expansion at China's expense elsewhere. But in part it was because in the 1890's the Russians and the British improved their relations in the area, an improvement symbolized by Russian War Minister General Kuropatkin's report to the Tsar in 1900: "India in the twentieth century would be a burden for Russia. In Asia there is arising a struggle of the non-Christian regions against the Christian ones. In this struggle we are on the side of England."[11]

CHAPTER IV

Russian Imperialism in Victory and Defeat

"Russia, with her territory adjoining ours, aiming to nibble away our territory like a silkworm, may be considered a threat at our bosom."[1] This was the evaluation of the Russian menace to China given the Emperor Hsien-feng in 1861 by his chief foreign affairs counselors. Some 35 years later, in the mid-1890's, it was clear to many observers that Russia was done with nibbling and was looking forward to taking great mouthfuls of territory from China. Li Hung-chang, the wily diplomat who conducted much of China's foreign policy in the late nineteenth century, wrote sadly in 1896 that Russia wanted "to control us in all our home affairs."[2] United States Ambassador to Russia Clifton Breckinridge had been even more blunt a year earlier when he wrote Washington that "Russia is ready for the partition of China."[3] His judgment was sound. He had anticipated a policy which was stated in these terms by one of the highest—and most cautious—Tsarist officials of the time, Finance Minister Serge Witte:

The more inert countries in Asia will fall prey to the powerful invaders and will be divided up between them. . . . The problem of each country concerned is to obtain as large a share as possible of the inheritance of the outlived oriental states, especially of the Chinese Colossus. Russia, both geographically and historically, has the undisputed right to the lion's share of the expected prey. . . . The absorption by Russia of a considerable portion of the Chinese Empire is only a matter of time.[4]

New forces were stirring vigorously in both Russia and China in the years that ended the nineteenth century. In Russia the energies that had been liberated with the end of serfdom in the 1860's were reaching maturity and producing a flood tide of change. The country was industrializing rapidly, filling the cities with thousands of peasants turned proletarian and increasing the numbers and influence of the urban bourgeoisie. Influential figures around the Tsar were looking for new worlds to conquer, anxious to cover their names with glory and to find new markets for Russia's rising industrial production. Their thoughts turned naturally toward the Far East, where China's evident decay presented tempting opportunities. Count Witte's program hoped even for an eventual Russian protectorate over all China, to be achieved by a steady peaceful penetration which would culminate in the attainment of dominant influence over the Chinese court in Peking.

In China, ideas of reform and change were in the air. Farsighted men saw that, to survive, the country would have to imitate Japan by abandoning old ways and learning from the West the essentials for a strong modern state. But for the most part the conservatives lead by the Dowager Empress were in the saddle, fighting reform and change. These conservatives clearly saw the threat the forces of change posed to the continuance of the now very degenerate and Sinified Manchu dynasty. With little military power, the best that Chinese statesmen could do was to try to divide and conquer, to inflame jealousies and rivalries among the various Western imperialist nations so that China's interests might be served. But once the full extent of Chinese military weakness was revealed nakedly in the mid-1890's, this effort proved insufficient.

Korea in the 1880's provided an example of how the Chinese thought they might protect their patrimony. The hermit kingdom was nominally a vassal of China, but

Japan had penetrated the area in the 1870's and had won the opening of diplomatic relations and the opening of some Korean ports for Japanese merchant ships. China was not displeased, therefore, when in the early 1880's several Western nations also secured some rights in and made treaties with Korea. But the chief struggle was between China and Japan, the latter favored by those Koreans who wanted reforms and modernization. In late 1884 the Japanese organized a *coup d'état* in Seoul to put their own men in power, but this was put down by Chinese troops. Both sides poured troops into Korea and a war seemed in the offing, but in April 1885 the dispute was settled peacefully. Both sides agreed to withdraw their troops and to permit the Korean king to hire officers from some third power. That third power, not unexpectedly in view of the geographic situation, turned out to be Russia. The result was a secret Russian-Korean agreement in which the Russians offered Korea protection and military instructors in return for the lease of a port in southeastern Korea, Port Lazarev. Learning of this, the British moved quickly to try to prevent a Russian protectorate over Korea. The British navy occupied Port Hamilton, an island off the coast of southern Korea. In the diplomatic fracas that followed, the Koreans decided not to ratify the treaty, the Russians promised not to threaten Korea's independence, and the British withdrew from Port Hamilton. The policy of setting "barbarian against barbarian" had worked.

As the 1890's began, the chief thrust of Russian Far Eastern policy was concentrated upon a new and most important project: the Trans-Siberian Railroad designed to connect western Russia with Vladivostok. Military, political and economic reasons all played a role in this momentous decision. From the strategic point of view, the railroad would for the first time make it relatively easy to ship additional Russian troops and supplies to the Far East and thus to help defend it. Moreover, the railroad was looked upon as a means of increasing the strength of the Russian position in the competition with its rivals for influence and territorial gains in China. From the economic point of view, the railroad offered great possibilities for remedying the great weakness of Russia's trade with China. The nature of that weakness is vividly shown by the statistics. During a typical year of the 1880's, the value of Russian imports from China was more than ten times as great as the value of exports. The average annual trade deficit in these years was over 23,000,000 rubles. Russia bought large quantities of Chinese tea for its entire population plus large amounts of essential supplies for the inhabitants of the Russian Far East. But Russian goods had a hard time finding Chinese markets. Competitive Western European goods could be sold much more cheaply in China because they were delivered by the cheaper water route. By cutting the time and cost of delivering Russian manufactured goods from European Russia to China, the Trans-Siberian Railroad offered attractive perspectives for Russian manufacturers and merchants.

Once the decision to build the Trans-Siberian had been made, the problem of its route to Vladivostok immediately arose. If it followed the Russian border across Siberia, it would have to sweep north along the great bend of the Amur River and be longer by hundreds of miles than a railroad line following the straightest, shortest route. But the straightest, shortest route to Vladivostok would have to go through Manchuria, opening prospects for greatly increased influence in that rich area, as well as for savings on railroad construction costs. How was Russia to get permission to build a railroad across Manchuria? This problem was very much in the minds of Russian policy makers in the first half of the 1890's.

The opportunity for solving the problem was provided by the short war of 1894–1895 between Japan and China. The Japanese won easily, demonstrating China's military weakness more clearly than ever before. At the Shimonoseki peace conference, the Japanese demanded they be given Formosa, the Pescadores Islands and the area around Port Arthur in Manchuria's Liaotung Peninsula. Tokyo asked also for payment of a large indemnity by China and Chinese recognition of Korea's independence. Aroused by the prospect of Japanese intrusion into Manchuria, Russia's foreign minister wrote the Tsar in early April 1895 suggesting that Russia organize an international intervention against this Japanese encroachment. The foreign minister's note declared: "Our aim is twofold: acquisition of an ice-free port on the Pacific, and the annexation of a part of Manchuria as a right of way for the Trans-Siberian Railroad." Nicholas II replied: "Russia absolutely needs a port free and open throughout the whole year. This port must be located on the mainland (southeastern Korea) and must certainly be connected with our possessions by a strip of land."[5] The need for ports open to navigation all year round was of course an old theme in Russian history, one used to justify territorial expansion in Europe and Asia.

To realize these plans, Russia was to pose as the defender of China. Together with Germany and France, therefore, on April 23, 1895 Russia presented what was in effect an ultimatum to the Japanese, a demand that they renounce the Liaotung Peninsula or take the consequences. Deciding they could not afford to fight Russia, Germany and France, the Japanese agreed to give up the Liaotung Peninsula in return for an increased monetary payment from China. To help China pay the indemnity to Japan, a joint Franco-Russian loan was negotiated. The grandiose plans behind these moves were indicated by the charter of a new bank formed that same year, 1895. This Russo-Chinese Bank's charter looked forward to the time when it might coin money, collect taxes, secure railroad concessions and engage in other farflung operations throughout China. Much of the capital for the new bank came from the great French banks, but the Russo-Chinese Bank was, as a Russian diplomat noted, "in reality but a slightly disguised branch of the Russian Treasury."

Despite this good beginning for the Russian plans, matters did not go smoothly. For one thing, other powers were alarmed by the prospect of rapid Franco-Russian penetration of China. As a result, the Chinese were able to get a British-German loan to supplement the earlier Franco-Russian advance. Moreover, there was opposition in Russia to Witte's scheme for building a railroad across Manchuria. Most important, the Chinese in early 1896 were proving recalcitrant to Russia's suggestions as to how she should be rewarded for her help in 1895. By April 1896 the Russian ambassador in Peking reported home that his effort to get the Manchurian right of way had been fruitless, and it was necessary "to make the Chinese Government decisively understand that a refusal will directly result in the most disastrous consequences to China."[6]

The story was to have a happy ending for the Russians, however, when Li Hung-chang came to St. Petersburg to attend the coronation of Tsar Nicholas II. Under great pressure—including the offer of a bribe of $1,500,000—Li finally negotiated a secret treaty with Russia. This provided for a 15-year defensive alliance between the two countries to be operative in the event of Japanese aggression against Russian territory in East Asia, against China, or against Korea. The key point of this treaty was Article IV, which read:

> In order to facilitate for the Russian land forces access to the points under menace and to assure the means of existence, the Chinese Government consents to the construction of a railway across the Chinese provinces of Amur and Kirin in the direction of Vladivostok.

> The junction of this railway with the railways of Russia shall not serve as a pretext for any encroachment on Chinese territory, nor for an attempt against the sovereign rights of His Majesty, the Emperor of China.[7]

In September 1896 the contract for what was to be called the Chinese Eastern Railroad was finally signed between the Chinese government and the Russo-Chinese Bank. The Chinese tried to put many safeguards into this agreement. Even in the earlier St. Petersburg negotiations, Li had refused to give the railroad concession to the Rus-

sian government. Nevertheless, the railroad soon became
a major instrument of Russian penetration into Manchuria
since the railroad company itself quickly became only a
thinly disguised instrument of the Russian government.
St. Petersburg had scored a major triumph. This was to
become increasingly evident in later years, as all pretense
that the railroad was a joint Russian-Chinese venture was
almost completely dropped. The railroad company became
in effect a Russian colonial administration in Manchuria,
administering the large right-of-way territory through
which the rail line ran, operating its own strong police
force which constituted in effect a private army on
Chinese territory, collecting taxes and governing the cities
and towns which grew up along the railroad. What was
intended became evident even at the very beginning, when
the sale of shares in the Chinese Eastern Railroad Company was conducted in such a way that would-be individual
purchasers were shut out and the Russian treasury got
them all. Much of the money for actually building the
line, however, came from France in the form of loans.

The Russian successes naturally increased the appetites
of the other great powers, and the Germans acted ener-
getically in 1897. Using the murder of two German mis-
sionaries as an excuse, German forces occupied Kiaochow
in mid-November 1897. Shortly afterward, the Tsar decided
to seize Dairen and Port Arthur on the Liaotung Peninsula, the very same area the Russians had prevented the
Japanese from getting in 1895. Witte objected to this,
fearing the impact of Chinese anger on the Chinese Eastern
Railroad, but the decision was taken, nevertheless, and executed by Russia's Far Eastern fleet. Under subsequent Russian pressure, the Chinese government was compelled to
lease the territory to Russia for 25 years and to permit the
building of a branch line of the Chinese Eastern Railroad
from Harbin to Port Arthur and Dairen. France and
Britain moved similarly to get their share of the loot. The
process of partitioning China was in full swing. After the
event, Witte wrote: "Our seizure of the Kwantung region
was an act of unprecedented perfidy." Both hypocrisy and

bribery were used to facilitate the major Russian *coup* at Port Arthur. Thus, several times in late 1897 and early 1898 the Russian government assured the Chinese that the occupation was temporary, that the Russian fleet's only purpose was to protect China against German aggression, and that the Russians would withdraw as soon as the Germans got out of Kiaochow. The result of all this maneuvering and deception was that Russia extracted from China greater gains in this area in 1898 than St. Petersburg had prevented Japan from acquiring in 1895.

The partition of China appeared to draw nearer as the year 1900 approached and each of the contenders moved to tighten its hold over the section of China it had picked for its own. Spheres of influence were marked out and the Chinese government was forced to declare she would not "alienate" one or another province to any other foreign power but the one at whose bidding the Chinese were acting at the moment. France got the island of Hainan. Britain extended its hold over the Yangtze Valley. Japan won assurances about Fukien. Then, to make assurance doubly sure—or to try to, anyway—the British and the Russians in April 1899 recognized each other's spheres of influence. Under the pretext of agreement on zones for building railroads, the Russians recognized British dominance in the Yangtze Valley, while the British recognized Russian primacy in the area "north of the Great Chinese Wall." In this situation the United States naturally feared for the future of its trade, investments and other economic activities in a China which might soon become simply a collection of foreign colonies. Moreover, the United States itself had no leased ports or spheres of influence to guard. Therefore, Secretary of State John Hay announced the Open Door doctrine, aimed at giving American merchants and investors rights of access to Chinese markets equal to the access enjoyed by merchants and investors of the powers controlling the different spheres of influence and leased ports. The American Secretary of State had Russia very much in mind when he moved in this way to try to protect China's territorial integrity and American rights in

China. The Russians, it need hardly be added, were not pleased, but after some delay they agreed to the Hay idea in words at least, though some of the words were ambiguous.

Very important, too, were the Russian efforts in the late 1890's to make Korea a vassal state. The Japanese victory in 1895 had forced the Chinese to recognize Korean independence. Tokyo began to strengthen its influence in Korea under the cloak of supporting Korean reformers, provoking disturbances which induced the King of Korea in February 1896 to take refuge in the Russian embassy in Seoul. Despite Japanese opposition, this enabled the Russians to turn Korea into a virtual Russian protectorate for a time. Russian officers were sent to train the Korean army, lumber and mining concessions were granted Russians, and in May 1896 the Korean king was even induced to ask the new Tsar, Nicholas II, to place Korea formally under Russian protection. The Tsar agreed, but his foreign minister managed to persuade him not to make a decision that might mean war with Japan. The Korean king left the Russian embassy in February 1897 and continued to work with his former protectors. The Korean government formed in September 1897 had a pro-Russian chief and all seemed to be going as the Russian minister in Seoul, Alexis Speyer, wanted it. But early in 1898 the king turned against the Russians. When Speyer demanded the removal of some anti-Russian figures from the government, threatening otherwise to withdraw the Russian military instructors from Korea, the king rejected the demand and the officers had to leave. The newly opened Russian-Korean Bank was ordered closed. The Koreans were using the rivalry between Russia and Japan to try to obtain a maximum of independence for themselves.

These events coincided roughly with St. Petersburg's success in leasing the Liaotung Peninsula from China and thus getting for itself—as we have noted—a privilege Russia had denied Japan in 1895. St. Petersburg decided to soften the latter blow to Tokyo by concessions in Korea. The result was the Nishi-Rosen Protocol of April 1898 in which both parties recognized Korean independence and promised not to interfere in Korean internal affairs. The same treaty also gave Japan predominant economic rights in Korea, equivalent to a monopoly position. But the very next year the Russian government took over vast timber concessions in Korea from private Russian interests; these they expanded in 1901. The Tsar in the early 1900's was still determined to make Korea a Russian province. He was working with advisers who had outlined a fantastic scheme to him: the conquest of Korea by troops brought into that country in the guise of lumberjacks to work the vast timber concessions the Russian government had obtained. Korea, therefore, was another battleground in the Russian effort to seize as much of China's historic empire as possible.

In Russia at the beginning of the twentieth century, foreign policy was ultimately made by the Tsar. The high officials surrounding him were essentially advisers who could suggest policies, conduct wars of memoranda against each other and otherwise intrigue to gain the Tsar's adoption of their ideas. But once the Tsar had made his decision, all officials had to obey the line he had set or else leave their posts. We have noted the role of Witte in influencing policy; the Tsar also gave much attention to the views of War Minister General Alexei Kuropatkin, a hero of the conquest of Central Asia. In the decade from 1895 to 1905 Russia had three foreign ministers: in order, Prince Lobanov-Rostovsky, Mikhail Muraviev and Count Vladimir Lamsdorff.

In the late 1890's, Witte tended to be the most cautious of the Tsar's advisers on the Far East, urging concentration on economic penetration and avoidance of armed conflict. General Kuropatkin tended to be the most aggressive adviser, confident of the strength of Russian arms and willing to use them against a China whose weakness had been shown up in the Sino-Japanese War. It is characteristic of Kuropatkin that when he got news of the Boxer Rebellion in 1900, he was overjoyed. "I am very glad!"

he told Witte then. "This will give us an excuse for seizing Manchuria." He had dreams of repeating his Central Asian triumphs against China. Witte, troubled by long-range considerations, worried that "if we assault China with fire and sword, we are forever making China our sworn enemy."

But even Kuropatkin was put in the shade in the early 1900's by a new group of adventurous imperialists who caught the Tsar's ear and began influencing his policy. The group was led by Privy Councilor A. M. Bezobrazov, who dreamed of Russia ruling the entire yellow race. Among its most important members was General Eugen Alexeyev, reputedly an illegitimate son of Alexander II. The conflicts among these advisers and cliques produced confusion and bewilderment among both Russians and non-Russians. Ambassadors abroad and other high government officials frequently did not know what the Tsar's policy really was, and as a result often gave out misinformation based on ignorance (though at other times misinformation was disseminated deliberately). The anger this situation produced abroad was vividly mirrored by American Secretary of State Hay when he wrote President Theodore Roosevelt in 1903 about the difficulties of negotiating with Russia, and commented: "Dealing with a government with whom mendacity is a science is an extremely difficult and delicate matter. . . . We are not charged with the cure of the Russian soul and we may let them go to the devil at their own sweet will."[8] While the influence of different advisers rose and fell, and different cliques held the upper hand at different times, the decisive element was the determination of Nicholas II to spread the dominion of Russia in Asia as widely and as rapidly as prudently possible. It was to prove a very expensive determination, one which helped lay the groundwork for the end of the Romanov dynasty and the Tsar's own execution.

But neither the Tsar nor any of his advisers knew what lay ahead when the Boxer Rebellion reached its climax in 1900 and opened the door to what seemed to be great further advances. The Boxer movement was a primitive but powerful Chinese grassroots reaction against the nation's humiliation at the hands of foreigners and the growing impact of these strangers upon traditional Chinese life. The Boxer ideology combined genuine patriotism, nationalistic xenophobia and religious fantasy to produce a movement whose members felt it their holy mission to kill the foreigners and the Chinese converts to Christianity. Many Boxers believed naively that observance of Boxer rituals would guarantee each individual Boxer's personal immunity to bullets, knives, spears or other hostile weapons. It is still a curious point as to how the Boxers arranged their apparently often convincing public demonstrations of their supposed invulnerability to hostile weapons. When a Boxer was struck down by these weapons, it was explained that he had presumably failed to believe ardently enough or had made a mistake in carrying out the prescribed complicated ritual. Millions came to believe that the Boxers and their magic could rid China of the cursed foreigners. Among those who placed their faith in the Boxers for a time was the ruler of China, the Dowager Empress, a fact that was to have great international political significance when she put the Chinese armed forces on the side of the Boxers in 1900.

So far as the Russians were concerned, the Boxer Rebellion had two aspects. One, the less important, was participation in the international force which marched on Peking in mid-1900 and lifted the Chinese siege of the foreign diplomats and their legation quarter in that city. The second aspect was the Russian use of Boxer activity in Manchuria to put that whole rich province under Russian military occupation.

The allied force of almost 20,000 men who marched on Peking from Tientsin included about 4,000 Russian soldiers under General Linevich. The polyglot relief force was plagued by national jealousies, confusion, misunderstandings and other ills to be expected of such a hastily created enterprise. Moreover, when the Russians were the first to break into Peking, some of their glory-hungry allies smarted under this feat and accused them of duplicity in not keeping to the plan of campaign. There is dispute on this point, but one fact is clear: the Russians joined enthusiastically with all the allies in looting Peking. Count Witte wrote in his memoirs:

> It was rumored that Russian army officers took a part in the looting, and I must say, to our shame, that our agent in Peking unofficially confirmed these rumors to me. One lieutenant general, who had received the Cross of St. George for the capture of Peking [apparently General Linevich] returned to his post in the Amur region with ten trunks full of valuables from the looted Peking palaces. Unfortunately, the general's example was followed by other army men.[9]

Perhaps the most ironical incident of the looting was the Russian removal of the original text of the Russian-Chinese treaty of alliance from the bedroom of the Dowager Empress who had escaped from the city before its capture by the relief force. Later, Russian authorities returned the document to the Chinese as "evidence" that Russia remained faithful to the alliance.[10]

In November 1900 the Russian armed forces used their power to force the Chinese to give them a concession of land in Tientsin, an example immediately followed by Japan, Austria, France, Belgium and Germany. Russian ambitions in the heart of China were also vividly indicated when Russian armed forces seized the Peking-Tientsin and Tientsin-Shanhaikwan rail lines. This alarmed the other European powers, particularly Britain, and their pressure forced the Russians to surrender these key rail arteries.

Remembering the precedent of 1895, when Russia's demonstrative friendship for China paved the way for major Russian gains in Manchuria, Russia's allies were dismayed shortly after the siege of Peking diplomats had been relieved when the Russian minister announced the Russian troops would be recalled from Peking to Tientsin. Russia asserted that its only interest was to help restore order and a proper legal government in China. Thus the

Russians sought to distinguish themselves from the other "imperialists" with whom they had worked so closely in the preceding weeks. We must turn to Manchuria, however, to understand why St. Petersburg was so anxious to impress the Chinese with its friendliness.

The Boxer movement, and its temporary backing by the Peking government in mid-1900, had profound repercussions in Manchuria, where many of the native population hated and feared the Russian penetration. The railroads under construction there were attacked and badly damaged. Chinese troops attacked Russian ships on the Amur River, bombarded Blagoveshchensk on the Russian side of the river, and even burned down Russian churches in Manchuria. Panic-stricken, Russians fled the province into Siberia or into the Port Arthur area where Russian troops were stationed. At Blagoveshchensk, the local Russian authorities retaliated in a particularly dreadful fashion, driving several thousand Chinese—men, women and children—into the Amur, where they drowned. St. Petersburg moved swiftly to take military advantage of the situation thus created. Russian troops moved into Manchuria and within a short period controlled the entire province, having routed the Chinese forces easily. The stage seemed set for the annexation of Manchuria, or something close to it.

Russian intentions in Manchuria became even clearer in November 1900 when the local Russian commander, General Alexeyev, forced the local Chinese authorities under Tseng-chi to accept a humiliating agreement. This provided that, though Chinese civil administration was to be restored in Manchuria, Chinese troops should be disbanded and disarmed and their military supplies turned over to Russian authorities. The agreement also authorized the stationing of Russian troops along the railroad right of way as guards. This naturally alarmed the Chinese authorities in Peking, and even drew opposition from Witte in St. Petersburg. The Chinese leaked the contents of the Alexeyev-Tseng agreement to the West and it was

published in the *Times* of London on January 3, 1901,
provoking consternation and protest in Western Europe,
the United States and Japan. But the expansionists still
held the upper hand in St. Petersburg, a fact shown by the
contents of a draft Chinese-Russian treaty handed the
Chinese ambassador by Russian Foreign Minister Lamsdorff in February 1901. This new draft went even further
than the Alexeyev-Tseng agreement. It included such provisions as the requirement of Russian-Chinese consultation
over the number of Chinese troops to be permitted in
Manchuria after the Chinese Eastern Railroad was completed; prohibition of Chinese arms imports into Manchuria; the Russian right to secure the dismissal of any
high-ranking Chinese official in Manchuria; and Chinese
agreement to get Russian permission before giving any
other nation railroad, mining or other concessions in the
whole vast border area of China from Sinkiang through
Mongolia and Manchuria. The Chinese leaked these
new demands to the West and the international situation
promptly showed the effects of the shock. Britain, Germany and Japan advised the Chinese not to sign the
treaty. Threats of war against Russia began to be heard,
especially from Japan.[11]

Li Hung-chang, who was directing China's foreign policy,
was playing a complicated game. Having been promised
a million-ruble bribe by the Russian government, he put
on a show of advocating signature of the Russian draft
agreement; the other powers all regarded him as a paid
Russian agent. But at the same time he told the British
representative that the Chinese government would be willing to communicate the Russian demands "and place
itself in the hands of the powers for protection against
Russia, whose demands it could not deny and whose
constant threats terrified it." Japan in particular seemed to
be anxious to go to war to prevent the Chinese capitulation
to the Russian demands, but the other major powers also
urged the Chinese to refuse their signature and in various
ways communicated their displeasure to the Russians. The
result was a Russian retreat. First they presented a re-

vised draft in which, for example, the Chinese commitment to give no concessions to other powers was limited to Manchuria rather than to the entire Sino-Russian border area of Manchuria, Mongolia and Sinkiang. Finally in April 1901 the Russians gave up completely for the moment. Count Lamsdorff announced that the draft treaty was being withdrawn and denied that Russia had ever had any desire to violate China's sovereignty or territorial integrity. He denounced the interference of other powers and said that Russian troops would remain in Manchuria until China had a more stable government able and willing to negotiate a treaty for withdrawal of Russian troops. The Russians had been checkmated for the moment in their efforts to get further legal rights in China, but their troops still ruled Manchuria.

The alarm raised among the other powers by this Russian maneuvering did not end, and its most concrete result was the Anglo-Japanese Alliance of January 1902, a treaty aimed at curbing Russian imperialism both in China and in Korea. Its immediate implication was that Russia would have to go to war with both Japan and England if it sought to continue its drive for Manchuria along the lines of late 1900 and 1901.

Shortly before the Anglo-Japanese Alliance, in the fall of 1901, the Russians had been negotiating with Li Hung-chang what finally seemed like an acceptable treaty. This provided for the withdrawal of Russian troops from Manchuria by 1902 and included permission for Chinese troops to be in Manchuria. But at the last moment the Chinese were told they would have to sign a secret agreement giving the Russo-Chinese Bank what amounted to a monopoly on the economic development of Manchuria. The Russians offered a 300,000 ruble bribe to Li if he would agree, but he stormed that "he could never dare to accept the responsibility for such an agreement which gives over to the Bank all Manchuria." Li died suddenly on November 4. The American envoy in Peking reported to his government that only a few hours before Li's death, the Russian minister went to Li's house and tried to have the official seals affixed on the treaty in the presence of the dying statesman, but he had come too late since the seals had already been given to another official. Early in 1902 the United States learned that the Chinese government was prepared to sign an agreement for evacuation of Russian troops which would give the Russo-Chinese Bank exclusive privileges for industrial development in Manchuria. The United States protested vigorously; Secretary of State Hay went so far as to say that if these privileges were granted, the United States "would be left in a position so painful as to be intolerable." This fervent United States opposition, together with the threat posed by the Anglo-Japanese Treaty, left the Russians no choice but to drop the demand for the bank to have these special privileges. The Russian-Chinese agreement finally signed on April 8, 1902 was far better for the Chinese than any earlier version. In this treaty Russia recognized Chinese sovereignty over Manchuria and promised to withdraw her troops from Manchuria in three stages over a period of 18 months. The reoccupation of Manchuria by Chinese troops was permitted, but only after the Russians had agreed as to the number of these troops and where they might be stationed.

From the Russo-Chinese Treaty of 1902 to the outbreak of the Russo-Japanese War in February 1904, the formation of Russian policy toward China was dominated much of the time by the fierce struggle at the apex of Russian power in St. Petersburg. Witte, supported increasingly by Foreign Minister Lamsdorff and even by General Kuropatkin, the defense minister, was for a relatively cautious policy of economic infiltration into China. Witte wanted to avoid war with Japan, and was even willing to sacrifice Korea to Japan. The palace clique of adventurers under Bezobrazov, which included the influential interior minister, Plehve, favored a much bolder policy.

Bezobrazov wrote the Tsar: "The Far East is still in a period when a stubborn struggle is necessary in order to assure the consolidation of our realm; domination by us is

the ultimate aim of this struggle; without such domination
we are not able either to rule the yellow race or control
the inimical influence of our European rivals." The Bezobrazov group used its influence to stall the evacuation of
Manchuria and to put new demands before China.

The first stage of the evacuation took place smoothly
on October 8, 1902, but at Newchwang in Manchuria
Russia continued to supervise the customs, the local administration and the judiciary, and to collect taxes. At
other Manchurian ports, the Russians set up their own independent customs service. The second stage of the
evacuation, scheduled for April 1903, did not take place.
Instead, the Russian minister in Peking, Lesar, presented
a list of seven new demands to the Chinese. The Russians
demanded that no additional treaty ports or foreign consuls
be allowed in Manchuria, that no foreigners other than
Russians be employed in the North China public service
and that no territory in Manchuria be transferred to any
foreign power. The Chinese made these demands known to
the West, and the United States, Britain and Japan denounced the Russian conditions, simultaneously warning
China not to grant them. Count Lamsdorff categorically
denied to the American ambassador that any such demands had been made. It was this denial which made
Secretary of State Hay explode about Russia having a
"government with whom mendacity is a science." The
United States was vitally interested because it wanted the
opening of Manchurian ports to American ships and trade.
The Chinese said they would be glad to grant the United
States' desires, but that the Russians would not let them
and would use any such action as an excuse for not with-
drawing their troops. Russian Ambassador Cassini in
Washington, on the other hand, said his country had no
objections. This was a game of diplomatic doubletalk.

The basic decision on Russian policy in Manchuria was
made after a special conference on February 7, 1903 between the Tsar and his advisers. Witte and Lamsdorff
demanded agreement with Japan and withdrawal of Russian claims to Korea and southern Manchuria, but the

Tsar decided against them. On July 30, 1903, he named General Alexeyev to a new post, viceroy of the Far East. This removed Far Eastern policy and armies from the jurisdiction of the ministers of foreign affairs and war, and put them instead under one of the key members of the imperialistic Bezobrazov clique. In effect two rival Russian governments existed, each intriguing against the other for the Tsar's favor. It was an ideal situation for confusion.

At about the same time in the summer of 1903, the Japanese suggested joint consultation about the two countries' Far Eastern interests. Tokyo submitted a draft treaty providing nominally for respecting the independence and territorial integrity of China and Korea. But the crux of the proposal was a section calling for reciprocal recognition of Japan's "preponderant interests in Korea and Russia's special interest in railway enterprises in Manchuria, and of the right of Japan to take in Korea and of Russia to take in Manchuria such measures as may be necessary for the protection of their respective interests." This set off a bitter fight in St. Petersburg between those like General Kuropatkin who thought the proposed treaty was acceptable and the members of the Bezobrazov clique who were determined not to surrender Russian designs on Korea.

The United States was involved in all this, too, because it was pressing China to sign a trade agreement which would open Mukden and Antung to foreign trade and permit the appointment of American consuls in Manchuria. Russian opposition was so intense that United States Minister Conger wrote the State Department despairingly: "What's the use? Russia is too big, too crafty, too cruel for us to fight. She will conquer in the end. Why not give up now and be friendly?"[12]

The date for complete Russian evacuation from Manchuria, October 8, 1903, was ignored by St. Petersburg, but the signing of the Chinese-American commercial treaty regarding Manchuria on that day brought howls of protest from the Russian expansionists. From Port Arthur, General Alexeyev's group assailed the agreement as "unfriendly and undiplomatic." Bezobrazov himself declared Russia intended to remain in Manchuria and "had no idea of permitting other nations to have equal commercial privileges with Russia there." These influential figures brought the same spirit into the negotiations with Japan. The Japanese amended their original proposal and suggested a neutral zone along the Manchurian-Korean border. The Bezobrazov group fought determinedly against even the modified Japanese position, refusing to give up the Yalu lumbering concession in Korea for which such high hopes were held. As a result the Tokyo proposals were rejected, but the Tsar wanted to continue negotiations and hoped to avoid war. The Russians' arrogance, their refusal to make significant concessions and their obstinate maintenance of illegal forces in Manchuria finally convinced the Japanese they could hope for no deal with St. Petersburg. On February 8, 1904, the Japanese fleet off Port Arthur began the Russo-Japanese War with a surprise attack on the Russian ships anchored off the port. If Americans had remembered this event, they might have avoided a similar Japanese surprise attack at Pearl Harbor on December 7, 1941.

Rarely has a nation miscalculated as completely as the Russian government did in the Russo-Japanese War. One of those who had favored the war, reactionary Minister of Interior Plehve, had declared: "We need a small victorious war to stem the tide of revolution." But the war actually helped bring on a near-revolution in 1905 and speeded up the decay of the Tsarist system. Its generals and admirals were shown to be incompetent; scandals in connection with troops and supplies exposed the corruption in the bureaucracy; and military defeat followed military defeat on both land and sea. We need not go into details of the war here. Suffice it to say that much of the land fighting between Russian and Japanese troops took place in Manchuria where the Russians suffered defeat time and again. Port Arthur surrendered on January 1, 1905. The great battle of Mukden in February and March, involving a total of 750,000 combatants, ended in Japanese victory. The final blow to Russian military hopes came in May 1905 when the Russian Baltic fleet arrived in the Pacific and was annihilated by Admiral Togo's forces at Tsushima. At home the war was widely unpopular among the Russian masses. Defeatist sentiments were very common among leftist and liberal forces. When Father Gapon led a workers' march on the Winter Palace, the demonstrators were met by a barrage of bullets. This outrage set off a wave of political strikes and agrarian disturbances which ultimately forced the Tsar to grant the first Russian Constitution and the establishment of the Duma.

Witte and Rosen represented Russia at the negotiations which began with Japan in Portsmouth, New Hampshire on August 9, 1905. The final peace treaty signed there showed what a major victory the Japanese had won. Russia recognized the paramount Japanese political, military and economic interests in Korea; Russia also agreed to withdraw its troops from Manchuria, and, subject to China's consent, transferred the Liaotung Peninsula lease—including Port Arthur and Dairen—to Japan, which also got free of charge the Russian-built railroads in the south of Manchuria. Russia ceded the southern part of Sakhalin Island to Japan and gave Japanese citizens fishing rights in the seas adjacent to Russia in the Pacific. The whole Russian Far Eastern drive, begun so brilliantly in 1895, seemed to have collapsed.

CHAPTER V

Tsarist Russia's Last Gains

For both Russia and China, the years 1905–1917 were tumultuous. In Russia the period began with an unsuccessful revolution and ended with two successful ones, the first of which toppled the Tsar while the second installed Bolshevik power. In China these were the years in which the centuries-old Manchu dynasty met its doom and was replaced by a weak and strife-ridden republic. But from the point of view of Russian-Chinese relations, the chief theme of this period was the same as earlier. Russian territorial encroachment on China continued as before, actually making some of its major gains in the years just preceding the end of the Romanov dynasty. Anyone who thought in 1905 that Russia's defeat by Japan and the extensive concessions made to Tokyo in the Treaty of Portsmouth spelled the end of St. Petersburg's pressure on China soon learned differently. What changed after 1905 was the direction of Russian pressure for new gains at China's expense; at the same time St. Petersburg used these years to improve and strengthen its position in northern Manchuria, the area in which the Russian presence was permitted to remain by the provisions of the Portsmouth Treaty.

The key to the 1905–1917 period was Russian-Japanese cooperation. Though strained at times, this cooperation dominated both countries' relations with China. The two countries moved together, aiming to divide northern China between themselves while fighting off both Chinese resist-

ance and possible competitive encroachment by other
powers, notably the United States. In Tokyo and St. Petersburg there were influential men who saw that in defense-
less China's huge territory and resources there was more
than enough for both nations, if they would work together
rather than fight each other. The Japanese wanted Russian support as they turned Korea into a colony and
fastened their hold more securely on southern Manchuria.
The Russians wanted similar Japanese backing as they
turned northern Manchuria into virtually a Russian colony
and started extending the colonization process into other
areas of northern China adjacent to Russian borders. Each
country distrusted the other, of course, and kept a sharp
eye out to make sure the other did not make any unexpected gains. Rivalry and jealousy between them went
hand in hand with cooperation.

Four secret Japanese-Russian treaties—in 1907, 1910,
1912 and 1916—spelled out the details of the two nations' alliance against China and against others who would
rival them in feeding off North China. The 1907 agreement saw Japan recognize Russia's primacy in northern
Manchuria and Russia's "special interests" in Outer Mongolia, while Russia promised to respect Japan's primacy
in Korea and southern Manchuria. In the 1910 agreement
each side gave the other a free hand in its assigned portion
of Manchuria, and both sides agreed to take "common
action" should either's "special interests" in Manchuria be
threatened. The 1912 agreement provided for the definition of the two powers' spheres of influence in Inner Mongolia. The 1916 agreement reached during World War I
provided for an alliance against any third power "which
may be hostile to Russia or Japan" and which might
threaten to win political dominance over China. The
treaty was certainly aimed at Germany, and probably also
at the United States.

One of the key factors driving the Russians and Japanese
together during this period was their fear of the United
States, which they saw striving for major economic and
political penetration of Manchuria. A moving spirit in

these American efforts was young Willard Straight. As American consul in Mukden from 1906 to 1908 he tried to arrange massive American investment in Manchuria, arguing this would both help protect China's territorial integrity and serve the interests of the United States. Another key figure was American railroad magnate Edward H. Harriman. The latter, whose son W. Averell Harriman was to play a key role in Soviet-American relations a half century later, envisioned a great globe-circling transportation system which would be facilitated by American ownership of either the Trans-Siberian Railroad, the Japanese-owned South Manchuria Railroad, or both. J. P. Morgan and Company and Kuhn Loeb and Company were also involved in these efforts, which had sympathetic support from the Taft administration. President Taft himself had declared that American foreign policy in the Far East "may well be made to include active intervention to secure for our merchandise and our capitalists opportunity for profitable investment which shall inure to the benefit of both countries concerned."[1] These efforts failed, primarily because the Russo-Japanese partnership effectively kept Manchuria a preserve for those two nations and their financial and commercial interests.

In China the key event of this period was the fall in 1912, after more than 250 years of power, of the Manchu dynasty. The men who led this revolution were moved very largely by nationalistic motives. They were appalled by the degeneracy and incompetence of Manchu rule, and they resented bitterly the repeated humiliations China had received at foreign hands. Sun Yat-sen and other revolutionary leaders dreamed of a new China, militarily, politically and economically strong, which could take what they considered its rightful place in the world community.

But the immediate impact of the revolution was fighting, disunity and fragmentation of political power over the country. To the greedy foreign powers watching the developing events, the Chinese Revolution seemed to offer new opportunities for further gains at China's expense. The

Russian foreign ministry made this judgment as events unfolded: "From the point of view of our interests, the dissolution of the present Chinese Empire would be desirable in more than one respect. Even in the event that various parts of China will not become entirely independent, there will develop between them a rivalry which will weaken them."

Russia took advantage of China's weakness before and after the fall of the Manchus to buttress its position in northern Manchuria. The result was described in these words by a Russian general in 1914:

> The Chinese Eastern Railway Administration represents, in the full sense of the word, a *colonial government* with all functions inherent to it. The manager of the railway administers at the same time the territory of the zone together with its population through all branches and in all respects; he is even endowed with the power of diplomatic relations, for which there is a special department in the structure of the administration.[2]

There was complete Russian political and economic control of the railway zone through Manchuria and the extensive lands adjoining the railway and annexed to the zone. Russian laws and Russian courts functioned in the zone; police and military power were in the hands of Russians, and a great new Russian city grew up at Harbin, the key station on the line. Using the railroad as a base, the Russians pressed economic penetration of Manchuria as rapidly as possible. Russian ships won the right to use the extensive Manchurian river system, and the Sungari River traffic became an important part of the Chinese Eastern Railroad's activities. The railroad opened up numerous coal mines and lumbering camps in Manchuria, too, and operated a large network of schools, libraries and clubs throughout its zone as well. This was a Russian empire within China, complete with a large-scale missionary enterprise aimed at disseminating Christianity among the Chinese.

The opening up of northern Manchuria by the Russian

railroad had major consequences, however, which St. Petersburg may not have anticipated and which increased concern among many Russians as time went on. About 2,000,000 people lived in northern Manchuria in the 1890's; by 1914 the figure was about 8,000,000. All but about 100,000 or 200,000 of these were Chinese attracted by the new economic opportunities created in the wake of the railroad, which could bring the area's products quickly and cheaply to markets. Chinese farmers began to work the soil, and the soybean soon became a major export crop. And as Chinese settlers moved north of the railroad and began farming the areas near the Russian border, the possibilities this opened for the future began to trouble some officials. One former manager of the railroad complained that his country had spent 800,000,000 rubles to settle 200,000 Russians and 15,000,000 Chinese in Manchuria. In southern Manchuria, where the Japanese-sponsored economic development was even more intensive, the Chinese population grew still more rapidly. Manchuria as a whole had had about 8,000,000 people in 1890; by 1920 it had 23,000,000.

We need not enter here into the detailed maneuvering by which the original Russian private railroad concession for Manchuria granted by Li Hung-chang in 1896 became the Russian economic empire and Tsarist colonial area of 1914. Suffice it to say that the tactics were no prettier than similar imperialistic ventures elsewhere. The Russians stretched their legal rights to the maximum and then exceeded them. They could do so successfully during these years because neither before nor after the Chinese Revolution could China resist successfully. The balance of power favoring the Russians was too uneven.

The most directly favorable impact of the Chinese Revolution, from Russia's point of view, was felt in Outer Mongolia. As we have seen, the boundary between Russia and Mongolia had been fixed in the Treaty of Kyakhta in the early eighteenth century. The next two centuries there were relatively quiet since the Chinese regarded this vast,

arid region as a buffer zone between China and Russia.
The relatively primitive Mongol people lived as nomadic
herdsmen in a feudal society which was ruled by princes
claiming descent from Genghis Khan as well as by Buddhist religious leaders. The prevailing Lamaism had turned
a large fraction of the Mongolian adult males into monks
living a life the very antithesis of that led by their ances-
tors, who had once conquered almost all of Europe and
Asia. Small colonies of Chinese merchants living in the
few cities of the region handled much of Mongolia's trade
and exercised powerful economic influence through credits
extended to the poverty-stricken herdsmen. About 5,000
Russians lived in the area before the Chinese Revolution,
engaging in trade against the Chinese competition, operating some leather factories and trying to exploit gold de-
posits.

Russian expansionist intentions toward Mongolia were
expressed most frankly about 1910 by the *Journal of
Commerce and Industry,* the organ of the Russian indus-
trialists:

Mongolia and Northern Manchuria naturally gravitate,
geographically and economically, toward Russia. . . .
We must do business there and control their markets.
Moreover, our frontier with China is unnatural, sinuous,
difficult to defend, and completely contrary to physico-
geographical conditions. A natural boundary of Russia
should consist of the deserts of Mongolia (Gobi). Those
lifeless seas of sand can be compared to the oceans
which separate peoples and states. Also two different
and absolutely incompatible races, like the yellow and
the European, ought to be separated by real obstacles to
a mass invasion. If we do not think about that at present, and if we allow the Chinese to control Mongolia
and Manchuria, then the roads which are to be con-
structed by them through the desert, close to us along
the Russian frontier, would be utilized to strengthen
their economic and political position to such an extent
that we Russians will be pushed backward to the Urals.[3]

Russian interest and increased activity in Mongolia after 1904 soon discovered fertile ground in the growing discontent of the Mongols. This was the product of increased Manchu activity in the area, which the native people saw as a threat. The key move was the decision to open Mongolia to Chinese settlement, followed by the beginning of systematic efforts to encourage large-scale Chinese colonization of Mongolia. Plans were also announced for stationing permanent Chinese garrisons in the area, for initiating Chinese mining enterprises, for a railroad and for a new Chinese industrial bank in Mongolia. Moreover, in 1910, a new Chinese *amban* or governor in Urga, capital of Outer Mongolia, began setting up a large network of government bureaus and schools. The Mongols did not like the prospect of increased Chinese immigration and tighter Chinese controls. The Mongol princes feared the lessening of their power as the new Chinese bureaucracy expanded. And all the Mongols disliked the new heavy taxes levied to support the burgeoning Chinese establishment. The Mongol leaders began to think of independence, of carving out a new vast Mongolian nation embracing all the related Mongol peoples. All this fitted in well with the Russian plans, and with the Russian fears that the new Manchu activity in Mongolia was primarily directed against the rising Russian influence there. Russian agents in Mongolia took care, therefore, to inflame this dissatisfaction and to encourage the Mongols to look to Russia for help in gaining independence from China. But there were also important voices to be heard in St. Petersburg about 1910 warning against too much involvement in Mongolian affairs and against excessive risks there.

It was with mixed emotions, therefore, that St. Petersburg received a delegation sent by the *khutukhtu* (living Buddha) and princes of Mongolia in August 1911. The delegation wanted Russian support for Mongolian independence and against Chinese efforts to change the status quo in Mongolia. A special conference of high Russian officials decided that it would be inexpedient to support

Mongolian independence, since this would involve complications which could divert Russian energies from Europe. But it was decided to support the Mongols in trying to maintain their own way of life and to protect the delegation and those who had sent them. A concrete measure taken was the sending of 200 Russian soldiers with machine guns to the Russian consulate in Urga. But the attitude of more ambitious Russian circles was typified by a Captain Makushek who was appointed to head the secret Russian convoy taking the Mongolian delegates home. He suggested using the Russian trading firms in Mongolia to set up a secret network of arms depots there. He proposed following this with the organization of partisan detachments which would stage an armed demonstration making possible the seizure of power in the area.

It was the activists who won out in the months that followed. Encouraged by the Chinese Revolution, the Mongols decided to revolt. They asked for and got from the Russians some 15,000 rifles, 7,000,000 cartridges, and 15,000 sabers in November 1911. The Russian war ministry, which had its Irkutsk military district deliver the arms, described the delivery as that of "private business firearms." At the beginning of December the Mongols carried out a *coup d'état* in Urga, disarming the small detachment of Chinese soldiers there and forcing the Chinese governor to take refuge in the Russian consulate, from which he was subsequently permitted to leave in Russian military custody for Peking via Siberia. On December 16, the formation of a new independent "Empire of Mongolia" was proclaimed with the Urga *khutukhtu* as its head, administering a government of five ministries—war, foreign affairs, interior, finance and justice. All Chinese merchants were expelled from Mongolia at the same time.

Though Russian diplomatic pressure protected them against the weak new Chinese government that succeeded the Manchus in 1912, the Mongols were soon embroiled in bitter arguments with the Russians. The Mongols wanted a really independent all-Mongol state, combining Inner and Outer Mongolia, as well as the area of Barga in

Manchuria whose inhabitants had expelled the Chinese in January 1912 and submitted to the Urga *khutukhtu's* rule. But the Russians opposed union of Inner and Outer Mongolia since this development would conflict with their secret treaty commitments to Japan. Moreover, the Russians also opposed the efforts of the Mongols to establish diplomatic and other contacts with states besides Russia and China, fearing the entry of competitors for commercial and political influence in Outer Mongolia. It took hard bargaining to get the Russo-Mongolian Treaty of November 3, 1912 concluded, and the Mongols were no longer very happy about the friend and protector they had turned to. The treaty did promise that Russia would help Mongolia "preserve her present autonomy and also her right to keep her national army, forbidding entry to Chinese armies and colonization of her lands by the Chinese." Mongolia in turn gave Russian subjects extensive privileges to live and engage in economic activities anywhere in Mongolia. A Russian postal service in Mongolia was also agreed to in the treaty. No rights denied Russians could be given to citizens of any third power. Given the great disparity of economic and political development between Russians and Mongols, it is clear the treaty amounted to creation of a Russian political and economic protectorate in Mongolia.

The news of the Russian-Mongolian Treaty created a storm in China. The new Chinese government denied that any valid treaty could be entered into between Russia and a part of China. The Chinese foreign office refused to accept a copy of the treaty from the Russians. Mass protest demonstrations took place throughout China and both high officials and ordinary citizens demanded the dispatch of armed forces to win back Outer Mongolia, even at the risk of provoking war with Russia. A Chinese military buildup began on the borders of Outer Mongolia, but Russia warned Peking that entry of troops into Outer Mongolia would mean war. Feeling rose so high that the Chinese foreign minister had to leave his post and flee Peking to ensure his safety. But the hard reality was that China was in no position to challenge the Russians militarily. It had no alternative but to try to salvage as much as possible by diplomatic means.

Very hard bargaining followed between Russia and China. A draft treaty agreed to in May 1913 was rejected by the Chinese in July. But finally a Russian-Chinese Declaration was made in November; the document was far from palatable to the Chinese but it was accepted as the best possible by Yuan Shih-kai, who had established what amounted to personal dictatorial rule over China. The declaration represented an exchange of Russia's recognition of China's suzerainty—but not sovereignty—over Outer Mongolia in return for China's recognition of Outer Mongolia's autonomy, its right to carry on its own internal administration and to settle for itself all questions of commercial and industrial relations with other nations. The last provision in effect legalized the sweeping economic concessions the Russians had won a year earlier in their agreement with the Mongols. China promised to keep troops out of Outer Mongolia and to refrain from colonization, while the Russians promised to keep no troops other than consular guards there. China agreed to accept Russian good offices to help settle the question of its future relations with Mongolia. Territorial and political matters concerning Mongolia were to be settled at a tripartite Russian-Mongolian-Chinese conference. In effect, therefore, a joint Russian-Chinese protectorate over Mongolia was set up, one in which the Russians were the senior partners.

The Mongols were furious in their turn since this agreement provided neither for their full independence nor for the union of Inner and Outer Mongolia. To help soothe the Mongols, the Russians gave them three separate loans totaling over 5,000,000 rubles during 1913–1914. These were intended to pay for reorganizing the administration of Outer Mongolia and for establishing and arming a Mongolian army. To help assure repayment of the loans, the Russians insisted on and secured the Mongols' acceptance of a Russian financial adviser. This adviser, S. A.

Kozin, became virtual economic ruler of Outer Mongolia, exercising his functions with the help of an extensive staff of Russian experts. His work was subsequently aided by the formation of a Russian-controlled Mongolian National Bank which had a monopoly on the issuance of currency in Outer Mongolia.

This chapter of Outer Mongolia's history was finally wound up by the tripartite Sino-Russian-Mongolian Agreement signed in June 1915 at Kyakhta after nine months of negotiation. In effect, this incorporated the two earlier agreements, recognizing Outer Mongolia's autonomy under China's suzerainty. Mongolia was given the right to make treaties and agreements of an economic nature but could not make agreements with foreign powers on political or territorial matters. On the latter questions Russia and China had to agree through negotiations with Outer Mongolian participation. As a concession to China, the Mongols agreed that the ruler of Outer Mongolia should receive his title from the president of China. The legal framework was complete for an Outer Mongolia dominated by Russia but nonimally part of China.

In one corner of Mongolia, Russia played an even bolder hand at the time of the Chinese Revolution than it played in the rest of Outer Mongolia. This was the northwestern portion of Mongolia termed the Uryankhai district originally and later called Tannu-Tuva. The 60,000 nomadic Mongols there lived in a region roughly the size of Great Britain. They were even more backward than their fellow Mongols and even more vulnerable to the Russian penetration which began when Russian merchants entered the area in the 1860's. It reached a mass basis at the end of the nineteenth century when thousands of Russian peasants began migrating to the area, seizing or leasing land for their farms. Russian settlers and merchants in the area exerted pressure on St. Petersburg to annex the area, but the Tsar's regime was cautious. Its researchers had found China's legal claim to the area incontestable, and there was fear of adverse British reaction to any overt moves. Hence, for a time the Russian government contented itself with backing the esablishment of Russian cultural institutions in the area and with sending in a small number of troops.

The Chinese Revolution encouraged a new look at the problem, and the Russian embassy in Peking began urging vigorous action to annex the region. The Tsar agreed, and planning got under way despite the realization that such action would face opposition from both the Mongols and the Chinese. The latter, of course, regarded all of Mongolia as their territory and were still bitter over the Russian maneuvers in Outer Mongolia. The Mongols also regarded Tannu-Tuva as part of their realm. But Tannu-Tuva was too far from Peking for the Chinese to do anything about Russian plans there, and the Mongols were too weak and too dependent upon the Russians.

In 1913 two regional Mongol chiefs were persuaded to appeal to the Tsar to take Tannu-Tuva under his protection. After some debate in St. Petersburg, it was decided to establish a protectorate over the area rather than annex it outright. The plan, a Russian official wrote later, "consisted of the quiet occupation of the region by Russians and the acquisition of *de facto* possession." On July 4, 1914 the Mongol *amban* of the area pledged that Tannu-Tuva would have no independent contact with any other country, thanked the Tsar for accepting the role of protector, promised to submit to the Tsar all local disputes and begged the Russian ruler "to leave to our Uryankhai population their customs, the Buddhist religion which they practice, their way of life, self-government, ranks, and nomad camps, permitting no special alterations which would tend toward a loss of power." Shortly afterward World War I broke out, ending fear of foreign concern over Russian actions in the area. The result was the installation of virtually complete Russian control, including the adoption of Russian civil and criminal codes as the law of the area. Russian immigration into the region was stepped up, and the local Mongol pressure for incorporation into Outer Mongolia was fought ruthlessly. Outer

Mongolia's plea for permission to have its agents enter Tannu-Tuva was refused completely in 1916. On the eve of the Russian Revolution, Tannu-Tuva was for all practical purposes part of Russia.

On the border of Russia and Outer Mongolia in northwest Manchuria, the Barga area was the scene of other Russian intrigues aimed at taking advantage of China's troubles at the time of the revolution. The Barguts, a Mongol people, also felt threatened and feared for the future of their nomadic cattle-tending society as the bars to Chinese immigration were lifted. As in Outer Mongolia, it was the war of the nomad against the farmer all over again. Events reached a crisis in Barga in 1911 when the Peking government ordered all schools conducted in Chinese. This resulted in an uprising which swiftly expelled the Chinese troops and pledged allegiance to the Urga *khutukhtu*. The Russians supported the Barguts and effectively warned the Chinese republican government against sending troops into the area. But the Russians opposed the union of Barga with Outer Mongolia. Their plan was to keep the area a part of northern Manchuria, which they hoped to annex. Meanwhile the Russians exerted pressure on China to grant Barga autonomy and to give the Russians priority in any railroad building there. In 1915 China gave in to most of these demands and Barga became a "special district" of China; Chinese immigration was limited and Chinese troops could be sent into the area only after advance notice to Russia. Russian influence was dominant in the area when the situation was radically changed by the dramatic events of 1917.

In Sinkiang, too, the Chinese Revolution produced new Russian activity, including the sending of Russian troops into some parts of the area. China demanded the withdrawal of the Russian troops but again could do nothing effective about it. In reply the Russians demanded the withdrawal of Chinese authority from much of the area and the granting to Russians of the right to settle in the area, demands China rejected. But the real result of the Chinese Revolution was the effective severing of bonds between Sinkiang and Peking, with the result that the area's governor, Yeng Tseng-hsin, ruled with little check. Nothing dramatic happened in the area before the Russian Revolution set new forces into motion.

On the eve of the Tsarist regime's downfall in early 1917, northern Manchuria and Outer Mongolia were essentially Russian protectorates. Russian influence also played an appreciable role in Sinkiang, though a less important one than in the first two areas. Writing about that time, the great Chinese revolutionary leader Sun Yat-sen estimated that this vast Russian sphere of interest in China made up 42 per cent of the country's land area. Britain on the other hand had substantial influence over 28 per cent of China, and Japan and France each had spheres of influence over about 5 per cent of China's territory. But the Russian sphere was primarily an area of mountains, deserts and poor grasslands, a region supporting only 3 or 4 per cent of China's people. If the Romanov dynasty had survived, the likelihood that it would sooner or later have absorbed northern Manchuria, Outer Mongolia and Sinkiang into the Russian empire seems high. But the Romanovs did not survive as Russia's rulers beyond March 1917. And little more than six months later the Bolsheviks took power. The complications that this fundamental development introduced into China's relations with Russia will concern us for the rest of this history.

CHAPTER VI

Soviet Power vs. Chinese Nationalism in the 1920's

"When the next Chinese general comes to Moscow and shouts, 'Hail to the World Revolution,' better send at once for the G.P.U. [the Soviet secret police]. All that any of them wants is rifles."[1] These bitter and disillusioned words were spoken in the late 1920's by Michael Borodin shortly after his career as chief Kremlin agent in China had ended in an historic debacle. He was paying unwilling tribute to a Chinese general, Chiang Kai-shek, who had outwitted Stalin and administered a crushing defeat to Soviet designs in China. That defeat, inflicted in 1927, was the key event in Russian-Chinese relations between the Bolshevik Revolution and the outbreak of World War II.

In the Petrograd of November 1917, during the "ten days that shook the world," Lenin and his comrades can have given little if any serious thought to China. In the months that followed their seizure of power, these men were concerned with Europe primarily. There were the highly developed capitalist countries with their hordes of proletarians. In these countries, Marxist theory had predicted, Socialism would triumph first. Lenin and Trotsky waited, eager and impatient for revolutions in Germany, France and Britain to bring the beleaguered Bolsheviks of Russia much-needed help. They had no reason in those early months to harbor any great expectations about China. Its vast peasant masses—sunk in what Marx and Engels had called "the idiocy of rural life"—had been almost completely ignored in the earlier Europe-centered analyses of Marxist theoreticians. In China itself there were few, even among the scholars, who knew anything of the Socialist theories for which Lenin stood. But the passage of a few years was to change the perspectives in both countries. Soviet attention turned more and more to the East, particularly to China, as it became clear that the hoped-for European revolutionary triumph was a fantasy. And in China the Bolshevik Revolution soon came to seem like a beacon of hope and inspiration to a portion of the Chinese intelligentsia that had never before taken Marx or Marxism seriously. Thereafter the creation of a Chinese Communist party, completely ruled by Moscow in its early years, required but a small step.

It did not take long for the basic dilemma of Moscow's China policy to emerge. On the one hand the new Bolshevik rulers were the heirs of the Tsars, commanding a national state whose imperialistic aggression against China had won vast gains in Manchuria and other Chinese border lands as well as important privileges—concession areas in some key Chinese cities, Boxer indemnity payments and the like—in China proper. On the other hand, these same men saw themselves as leaders of a world revolutionary movement appealing to the oppressed and downtrodden everywhere. What should their attitude be toward those areas and peoples which had suffered from Russian imperialism and oppression?

The problems flowing from this dilemma were masked at first by the fact that Soviet weakness in Asia gave the Kremlin no practical possibility of seeking to defend Tsarist-won positions in China. Thus there were no initial barriers to a flow of public statements and declarations projecting an image of revolutionary fervor, idealism and zeal for justice and equality. In the early phases of the Russian civil war after 1917, after all, most of Siberia was held by Kolchak and other anti-Soviet Russian military leaders, as well as by Japanese, Chinese and American troops. In northern Manchuria, Chinese troops took over the Chinese Eastern Railroad zone with the help of the anti-Bolshevik Russian management. In Sinkiang and Outer

Mongolia, too, Chinese power was able to reassert itself in the vacuum left by the weakness of a Russia torn by bloody domestic strife. To Lenin and his colleagues, fighting for the revolution's survival in the heart of their country, the disappearance of Tsarist spheres of influence in China was initially a matter of little importance. They sought instead to turn the loss into a propaganda weapon.

Typical of this early Soviet attitude was the declaration issued by Deputy People's Commissar for Foreign Affairs Leo Karakhan on July 25, 1919 to the Chinese nation. This statement declared that the Soviet government early in its existence had called for negotiations with China "to annul the treaty of 1896, the Peking protocol of 1901, and all agreements concluded with Japan between 1907 and 1916; that is, to return to the Chinese people everything that was taken from them by the Tsarist Government independently, or together with the Japanese and the Allies." The heart of the Karakhan Declaration was contained in these paragraphs:

The Soviet Government has renounced the conquests made by the Tsarist Government which deprived China of Manchuria and other areas. Let the peoples living in those areas themselves decide within the frontiers of which State they wish to dwell, and what form of government they wish to establish in their own countries.

The Soviet Government returns to the Chinese people without compensation of any kind the Chinese Eastern Railway, and all mining concessions, forestry, and gold mines which were seized from them by the government of Tsars, that of Kerensky, and the outlaws Horvath, Semenov, Kolchak, the Russian generals, merchants and capitalists.

The Soviet Government renounces the receipt from China of the 1900 Boxer rebellion indemnity. . . .

The Soviet Government abolishes all special privileges and gives up all factories owned by Russian merchants on Chinese soil. Not one Russian official, priest, or missionary shall be able to interfere in Chinese affairs, and if he commits a crime, he should be subject to the justice of the local courts. . . .

If the Chinese people wish, like the Russian people, to become free and to avoid the fate which the Allies prepared for them at Versailles, a fate designed to turn China into a second Korea or a second India, they must understand that their only allies and brothers in the struggle for freedom are the Russian workers and peasants and their Red Army.[2]

This sweeping renunciation of Russia's imperialist gains in China was intended to, and did, arouse wide enthusiasm in China. But it is indicative of the confusion and difficulties reigning in the period that the recognized Chinese government in Peking did not receive the text of the Karakhan Declaration until March 1920, more than eight months after its release. The text received in Peking from a Soviet official in Siberia contained the second paragraph quoted above, a paragraph whose favorable impact on Chinese public opinion was particularly strong. But the official Soviet version of the declaration—published in August 1919—lacks this paragraph and Soviet sources have often denied that this renunciation of the Chinese Eastern Railroad was ever actually made. What seems to have happened is this: the paragraph was at least in an early version of the declaration, one drawn up when the battles in Siberia were not going well for the Bolsheviks. But later, when time came to publish the declaration, Soviet successes against Kolchak had so changed the situation that Moscow officials were far less ready to surrender historic Russian rights in the railroad than they had been earlier. Hence the paragraph was omitted in the published version.

Two years after the Karakhan Declaration, however, the Soviet government began following a policy of Outer Mongolia which looked to many Chinese like simply a repetition of the Tsarist policy of a decade earlier. The crudity with which Lenin's regime turned Outer Mongolia into the first Soviet puppet state was all the more glaring

because of the promises which had been made to the
Mongols in August 1919. Then, the Soviet government
had spoken in these terms to the people of Outer
Mongolia:

> The Russian people have renounced all treaties with the
> Japanese and Chinese governments which deal with
> Mongolia. Mongolia is henceforth a free country. Rus-
> sian advisers, Tsarist consuls, bankers and the rich who
> have mastered the Mongolian people by means of force
> and gold and robbed them of their last possessions must
> be driven out of Mongolia.

> All institutions of authority and law in Mongolia must
> henceforth belong to the Mongolian people. Not a single
> foreigner has the right to interfere with Mongolian
> affairs.[3]

The reality of the situation in Outer Mongolia in late
1919, however, was that Chinese rule had been reimposed
upon the area, and the dominating Russian position won
five years earlier had been essentially wiped out. Chinese
troops under General Hsu Shu-tseng had seized control of
Urga and forced the *khutukhtu's* government to petition
Peking to be readmitted to the Chinese republic. Not only
was Mongolia's autonomy ended but the Mongols were
disarmed, their use of Russian currency was prohibited,
and they were compelled to turn again to the use of
Chinese financial and trading services. Heavy taxes were
levied on the Mongols for the support of the Chinese
forces in the area, and they were dunned for the payment
of old debts—plus accumulated interest—owed Chinese
merchants at the time of the 1911 Mongolian revolt. The
Chinese policy, in short, was one ideally suited to alienate
the Mongols.

All this created a situation in which it became possible
for a strange adventurer, Baron Ungern Sternberg, to
rule briefly over Mongolia. A former Tsarist officer, the
baron entered Mongolia with a force of several thousand
troops in October 1920 after the larger Russian anti-Com-

munist army in which he had served had been defeated. His first attempt to capture Urga from the Chinese was repulsed, but late in 1920 and early in 1921 several thousand Mongols joined his army, seeing in it the means of liberating their country from Chinese rule.

The baron's forces captured Urga in February 1921, effectively and abruptly ending Chinese rule over Outer Mongolia. Sternberg's rule was brief but bloody and tinged with fantasy. His troops engaged in wholesale massacres of his opponents, and the baron himself dreamed of a career as a new Attila conquering Asia for the Asiatics, and then Europe for the fallen Hohenzollern and Romanov monarchies. Reality dealt harshly with this madman who had boasted that "with my Mongols I shall go to Lisbon." When he tried to invade Siberia, he was quickly defeated by Soviet forces, taken prisoner and executed, all before the year's end.

These events set the stage for the resumption of Russian control over Mongolia. A façade of legality was cast over the intervention by the creation of a tiny Mongolian People's Revolutionary party which met in the border town of Kyakhta in March 1921 and proclaimed a "Provisional Revolutionary Government of Mongolia." This "government" appealed for Soviet help to annihilate the baron's forces, help which was quickly and enthusiastically supplied. The Soviet forces and their Mongolian puppets marched into Urga in July 1921 and Outer Mongolia became the first Soviet satellite. A Soviet-Mongolian Treaty signed in November 1921 gave the Russians such privileges as the right to establish postal and telephone communications in Outer Mongolia and promised them the cession of land needed for the construction of railroads in Mongolia. In an effort to avoid Chinese anger, the treaty was kept secret for a time and a Soviet envoy in Peking, Alexander Paikes, directly denied that any such treaty had been concluded. When the fact of the treaty became clear, Chinese anger was very great. Soviet Russia appeared to be following Tsarist Russia's policy of trying to detach

Outer Mongolia from China. The bitter Chinese reaction was summed up this way in an official note of May 1922:

> The Soviet Government has repeatedly declared to the Chinese Government: . . . that the Soviet Government renounces all encroachments of Chinese territory and all concessions within China, and that the Soviet Government will unconditionally and forever return what has been forcibly seized from China by the former Imperial Russian Government. . . .

> Now the Soviet Government has suddenly gone back on its own word and, secretly and without any right, concluded a treaty with Mongolia. Such action on the part of the Soviet Government is similar to the policy the former Imperial Russian Government assumed toward China.[4]

The major significance of the Mongolian incident was that it marked the emergence of an active Soviet policy in relations with China. Gone were the times when Moscow had to accept diminution or elimination of the old advantages won by the Tsars because it was too busy defending Bolshevik power within Russia itself. Now the anti-Bolshevik forces had been largely defeated and economic strength was increasing again within Russia. Energy was now available for salvaging at least part of the old Russian power in China, and ambitions were being nursed in Moscow for achievements there far surpassing anything the Tsars had accomplished. The Romanovs had had only the conventional instruments of military power and diplomatic pressure to accomplish their aims. The Soviet state —as later events in the 1920's showed—had and could use these instruments, too. But in addition it had at its command a force of which the Romanovs never even dreamed: the attractive power of Communist ideology. The Chinese adherents of this ideology could be manipulated by the men in the Kremlin who simultaneously ruled both Russia and the Communist movement. The new concepts maturing in Moscow were summed up by Lenin's observation that "Russia, India, China, etc. contain a mighty majority of the population. And precisely this majority of the population is, with unexpected rapidity in recent years, being drawn into the fight for its own freedom." His conclusion was that this phenomenon meant "the final victory of socialism is fully and unconditionally secured."[5]

Chaotic conditions in China during the early 1920's offered the Soviet Union, both as a state and as the fount of the world Communist movement, rich opportunities. China in these years was an arena for the contending ambitions of several warlords and their private armies which controlled different portions of a divided nation. The government at Peking, recognized by foreign powers, exercised no real sovereignty beyond the area controlled by the warlord ruling there at any moment. A rival aspirant to national power existed in South China, at Canton, in the shape of a government often related to or headed by Sun Yat-sen and his Kuomintang. But Sun Yat-sen, too, was dependent on warlord favor. Among the intellectuals, nationalism was at a fever pitch. Angered by their country's repeated humiliation at the hands of foreign powers and convinced that China's traditional institutions were useless for meeting the needs of the twentieth century, the Chinese intelligentsia looked abroad eagerly for ideas and organizational forms that might permit the building of a new, strong and prosperous China. Among the urban masses, a new mood of militancy was evidenced by the spread of trade unions and the outbreak of major strikes. Lenin noted early in this period that "in China there is raging hatred against the Japanese, also against the Americans."[6]

For those who shaped Soviet strategy and tactics toward China in the early 1920's, the ultimate objective was a Communist China. But that seemed distant indeed in an overwhelmingly rural country, a nation where powerful foreign interests—notably those of Britain and Japan—existed. The course decided upon, therefore, was a three-pronged one aimed at securing immediate objectives while still laying the groundwork that might make possible the ultimate goal. Between 1921 and 1924 substantial progress was made by Moscow in all three major directions of its China policy.

Effort number one was aimed at normalizing Soviet relations with the internationally recognized Chinese government in Peking, establishing good relations with key warlords elsewhere, and generally cultivating the conservative forces in China. In pursuing this policy, Moscow had in mind winning back as much as possible of the old Russian position on the Chinese Eastern Railroad in the Manchuria controlled by warlord Chang Tso-lin, and also securing opportunities for the spread of Soviet influence in the areas controlled by these conservative elements. Among the northern warlords that Moscow wooed, the so-called Christian general, Feng Yu-hsiang, was particularly willing to be cooperative on a number of occasions. As a reward he received substantial stocks of Russian weapons and munitions for his troops and was given refuge in Moscow for a time during 1926.

A series of Soviet attempts to normalize relations with Peking failed during 1920–1923. The first effort had been made by M. I. Yurin, a delegate representing the Far Eastern Republic, a nominally independent and supposedly non-Communist state the Bolsheviks operated for a time in eastern Siberia. Yurin was able to get Peking to revoke its recognition of the old Tsarist diplomats, but he finally left empty-handed, frustrated by Chinese anger at the Soviet entry into Outer Mongolia. In December 1921 a mission formally representing Moscow arrived in Peking under the leadership of Alexander Paikes. Paikes also had to go home empty-handed in mid-1922; Chinese anger had exploded when his denial that a Soviet-Mongolian treaty had been signed was found to be false. Paikes was followed in August 1922 by the highest level Soviet diplomat to visit Peking, Adolf Joffe, a man nominally empowered to settle all issues in dispute. The Joffe mission began well, and Chinese public opinion was favorably impressed by a series of public statements, interviews and speeches Joffe gave emphasizing Russia's desire to help China against foreign imperialists and to respect fully China's sovereign rights. But the Chinese insisted that Russian troops evacuate Mongolia and that Moscow carry out what Peking regarded as the Karakhan Declaration's promise to turn over the Chinese Eastern Railroad to China. Joffe, too, therefore had to leave without any agreement. Only after Leo Karakhan himself—the author of the Karakhan Declaration of 1919 and of a similar statement issued in 1920—arrived in Peking in mid-1923 was it finally possible to resolve the impasse and reach an agreement, and then only after a half year of hard bargaining, some of it extremely ugly.

The Sino-Soviet Treaty Karakhan concluded in 1924 represented a major victory for Moscow. It was made possible by the steadily increasing Soviet strength and by the weakening position of the Peking regime, which found itself under heavy attacks from domestic enemies, some of them supported by the Russians. Events were to prove that the verbal concessions given the Chinese in the treaty were often meaningless in practice. The practical effect of the treaty was to give the Russians a substantial fraction of the rights in China which the Tsars had won, which had been temporarily lost in the chaotic early years following the Bolshevik Revolution. Many Chinese realized this and the Peking regime refused to ratify the first version of the treaty reached in negotiations between Karakhan and C. T. Wang. Karakhan's first reaction to the refusal was in the classic imperialist tradition. He gave the Chinese government a three-day ultimatum, warning that if the treaty were not ratified Russia would break off the negotiations and China alone would bear "the responsibility for all the ensuing consequences." The threat did not succeed fully, but negotiations were resumed and the final treaty differed only slightly from the original.

The key provisions of the new treaty were these: China and Russia resumed diplomatic relations. The Soviet government agreed to nullify all Tsarist agreements and treaties affecting the sovereign rights of China. The Soviet Union recognized Outer Mongolia as part of China's sovereign realm, and agreed to withdraw its troops as soon as various questions involved were agreed upon at a subsequent conference. The Soviet and Chinese governments would jointly administer the Chinese Eastern Railroad as a commercial enterprise, while the road's future would be more fully settled at the scheduled subsequent conference. The Soviet government agreed to renounce the Russian share of the Boxer indemnity and the former Russian extraterritorial rights in China, but it received certain consular, church and other Russian property in China.

Later, in September 1924, Karakhan signed a supplementary agreement in Mukden with the real master of Manchuria, Chang Tso-lin. This incorporated much of the earlier agreement, as well as some provisions covering points affecting the railroad, such as the setting up of a joint commission to dispose of the road's profits. Joint Sino-Soviet management of the railroad began on October 3, 1924. Karakhan now boasted openly of his triumph: "At present the Soviet Union is gaining a firm foothold in the Far East by occupying one of the most important positions of which its enemies were trying to deprive it. In addition to the political, economic and other advantages, the Soviet Union has recuperated [sic], on October 3, a property which according to the most conservative estimate is worth over a half billion rubles."[7]

The other two major Soviet policy lines in China during the early and middle 1920's were so closely interlinked that we may consider them together here. One line sought to and did create a Chinese Communist party subject to the discipline and direction of the Communist International headquarters in Moscow. The other line was the encouragement given to Sun Yat-sen's Kuomintang, a nationalistic, non-Marxist middle-class organization. The Soviet effort, which failed in 1927, was to provide organizational and material help to the Kuomintang so that it could ultimately gain control of all China in a situation

where it would be greatly indebted, and presumably
friendly, to the Soviet Union. Simultaneously the Chinese
Communists were instructed to join the Kuomintang and
gain as much influence and as high place in the Kuomintang as they could, looking forward ultimately to the time
when the Communists would displace the Kuomintang as
the masters of China. In this Soviet plan Sun Yat-sen—
and after his death Chiang Kai-shek—was to be the
Kerensky of China.

What was attempted in China was a particular application of the general tactics Lenin had spelled out in 1920,
at the Second Congress of the Communist International,
for use in the then vast colonial realm ruled by the West.
In this area, Lenin knew, there was virtually no proletariat
and the mass of the people were peasants. He saw the
middle classes in these countries struggling for national
independence, an objective in whose realization he believed Communists could profitably participate. But he
worried about the danger that the Communists might be
submerged in the ensuing united front and might therefore
be prevented from pursuing their own more revolutionary
ends, which must ultimately turn them against their bourgeois allies. Here is the way Lenin's Theses on the National
and Colonial Question, adopted by the Comintern in mid-
1920, put the matter:

> In regard to the more backward countries and nations,
> with prevailing feudal or patriarchal and patriarchal-
> peasant relations, it is especially necessary to bear in
> mind the following:
>
> (a) All Communist parties must give active support to
> the revolutionary liberation movements in these coun-
> tries. . . .
>
> (d) In backward countries it is especially important to
> support the peasant movements against the landowners,
> large-scale land ownership and all feudal survivals. . . .
>
> (e) It is likewise necessary to fight the attempts to
> cloak with Communist garb the revolutionary movements

for liberation in the backward countries which are not truly communist. It is the duty of the Communist International to support the revolutionary movements in the colonies and in the backward countries, for the exclusive purpose of grouping together the various elements of the future proletarian parties . . . in all the backward countries, and educating them to the consciousness of their specific tasks—i.e., the tasks of fighting the bourgeois-democratic tendencies within their respective nationalities. *The Communist International must be ready to establish temporary relationships and even alliances with the bourgeois democracy of the colonies and backward countries. It must not, however, amalgamate with it. It must retain the independent character of the proletarian movement, even though this movement be in the embryonic stage* [italics added]. . . .[8]

Even when Lenin presented these theses he met opposition from Communists who feared that their movement would lose by these tactics, and who wanted to focus on exclusive development of the Communist party in each such country. M. N. Roy, an Indian Communist who also played a prominent role later in China, led the opposition, but Lenin answered: "The Hindu Communists are duty-bound to support the bourgeois liberation movement, without, however, merging with it."[9] The issues thus raised in 1920 were to become of major importance a half decade later as the Soviet-supported forces in China surged forward and controlled more and more of that vast country. And the application of this tactic under Chinese conditions was to play a significant role in the Soviet power struggle between Stalin and Leon Trotsky.

A tiny group of intellectuals founded the Chinese Communist party at the beginning of the 1920's. Under the leadership of two Peking University professors, Chen Tu-hsiu and Li Ta-chao, the founders saw in Marxism-Leninism and the Soviet example the ideology and the pattern for a rebirth of China. These professors and their students were originally primarily nationalists, disillusioned and bitter with the West for what they regarded as the betrayal of China at the Versailles Conference. They saw the Soviet Union as the friend and helper of the exploited and oppressed colonial and semi-colonial nations such as China. Moreover, Lenin had won in Russia. Might not his tactics, his ideology and his program win in China? These were dizzying and inspiring perspectives for the professors and students who were the nucleus of the Chinese Communist party. Three decades later one of the student members of the group, Mao Tse-tung, became ruler of all mainland China as the head of the vast and powerful organization which had grown from this tiny start.

A major role in forming and shaping the new Chinese Communist party was played from the very beginning by a series of Communist International agents. The first to get results was a Russian, Gregory Voitinsky, who helped finance and form first the Chinese Socialist Youth Corps in August 1920 and then, a month later, the Chinese Communist party itself. The second was a Dutchman, Maring, who attended the party's first congress in July 1921 and made a deal with the current Peking warlord of the time, Wu Pei-fu, which gave the Communists free organizational rein in the area in exchange for Communist support of Wu against his warlord rivals. These pioneers, Voitinsky and Maring, and the men who came from Moscow after them in the 1920's trained the Chinese Communists in Marxism-Leninism, transmitted Moscow's orders on strategy and tactics, and generally acted as ideological and political governors of the party. However, the contempt that many in Moscow felt for the fledgling Chinese Communists was vividly expressed in 1922 by Karl Radek at the Fourth Comintern Congress:

The comrades working at Canton and Shanghai have failed to associate themselves with the working masses. . . . Many of our comrades out there locked themselves up in their studies and studied Marx and Lenin as they had once studied Confucious. . . . You must understand, comrades, that neither the question of socialism nor of the Soviet republic are now the order of the day. . . . The immediate task is: (1) To organize the young working class; (2) To regulate its relations with the revolutionary bourgeoisie elements in order to organize the struggle against the European and Asiatic imperialism.[10]

The "revolutionary bourgeoisie elements" Radek and his fellow Muscovites had in mind were the members of the Kuomintang under Sun Yat-sen, who had briefly a decade earlier been the first president of the Republic of China. As early as 1912 Lenin had praised Sun Yat-sen's ideas, seeing him as a leader of the progressive bourgeoisie anxious to break the grip of both foreign imperialism and native feudalism on China. Sun's ideas of nationalism, democracy and economic welfare owed much to his study of Western history and institutions, and he was certainly not a Marxist. But Sun and his followers had prestige and fame in China in the early 1920's, and therefore political potentialities far exceeding anything the infant Chinese Communist party could claim at the time. Moscow calculated that if the Kuomintang's military, organizational and political weaknesses could be rectified, Sun Yat-sen and his followers could be made the rulers of China. And if the Chinese Communists played their cards right in working with Sun, so Moscow reasoned, Sun would prove only a transitional figure and the way would have been prepared for the Red flag to fly over all China. To accomplish this goal, the first steps were clearly to persuade Sun to work with the Communists and with Russia, and to induce the Chinese Communists to work with Sun. In the first case, Sun's antipathy to Marxism and his distaste for the Russian moves in Outer Mongolia had to be overcome, a task which was eased by the lack of interest the Western powers showed in helping the Kuomintang. In the second case the Kremlin had to overcome the Chinese Communists' reluctance to work with a bourgeois leader and the preference of many of them to concentrate on building up the Communist party. The Chinese Communists' objections to collaboration with the Kuomintang ended only after their unhappy experience in the Peking area where warlord Wu Pei-fu's soldiers destroyed the alliance with the Communists by massacring a group of railroad workers the Communists had organized. This helped convince them that the working class movement in China was too weak to try to remake their country alone.

The chance of persuading Sun to work with Russia improved in November 1921 when the Comintern agent Maring briefed the Kuomintang leader on the latest developments in Moscow's realm. Here is how Sun described the impact of this meeting on him:

I had been very skeptical that Marxism—pure Communism—could be carried out after the Soviet revolution . . . Russian industry and commerce are not very developed, and Communism, unable to succeed in isolation, still has a long way to go to be realized. Now I have just learned from Maring that Soviet Russia, after having a go at Communism, ran into deep difficulties and therefore switched to the New Economic Policy. The spirit of this New Economic Policy coincides with the Principle of People's Livelihood which I advocate. I am very glad that Soviet Russia has embarked on a policy which corresponds to my principle and am strengthened in the belief that my principle can be entirely realized and must ultimately succeed.[11]

Negotiations with Sun continued during 1922. He was suspicious of the Communists and wanted to be sure he would not be harboring a Trojan Horse if he collaborated with them. He told Maring at a later meeting: "If the Communist party enters the Kuomintang, it must submit to discipline and not criticize the Kuomintang openly. If the Communists do not submit to the Kuomintang, I shall expel them; and if Soviet Russia should give them secret protection, I shall oppose Soviet Russia."[12]

The negotiations were finally concluded in January 1923 when Adolf Joffe and Sun Yat-sen reached agree-

ment that members of the Chinese Communist party would
be admitted to the Kuomintang. Their statement said:

> Dr. Sun Yat-sen holds that the Communist order, or
> even the Soviet system cannot actually be introduced
> into China, because there do not exist here the condi-
> tions for the successful establishment of either Com-
> munism or Sovietism. This view is entirely shared by
> M. Joffe, who is further of the opinion that China's
> paramount and pressing problem is to achieve national
> unification and attain full national independence, and
> regarding this task he had assured Dr. Sun Yat-sen
> that China has the warmest sympathy of the Russian
> people and can count on the support of Russia.[13]

Joffe also pledged Russia to renounce all Tsarist treaties,
while Sun agreed to back a "temporary" reorganization of
the Chinese Eastern Railroad under joint Sino-Soviet
management. Joffe assured Sun that Russia had no imperialistic aims in Outer Mongolia and would not "cause
it to secede from China." Sun accepted this and responded
that immediate evacuation of Russian troops from that
area was not "either imperative or in the real interest of
China."

Events moved swiftly to get results from the tripartite
Soviet Russia–Kuomintang–Chinese Communist party alliance. That summer of 1923 Sun Yat-sen ordered his
young aide, General Chiang Kai-shek, to go to Moscow,
learn what he could there and negotiate for Soviet military
assistance. When Chiang returned, he became head of the
Whampoa Military Academy whose function was to train
officers for the Kuomintang army. To help the academy,
Moscow provided 3,000,000 rubles as well as some 40
Soviet officers as instructors and advisers for a curriculum
which combined political indoctrination with technical
military training. At least equally important was the arrival of Michael Borodin in China in September 1923.
Nominally a correspondent for the Soviet news agency
Rosta, he was actually intended to be chief adviser to
Sun Yat-sen. His task was nothing less than the complete

remolding of the Kuomintang and its forces along strictly centralized and tightly disciplined Soviet lines, thus revolutionizing this hitherto loosely organized and extremely weak organization. Borodin, who had once been a school principal in Chicago and whose chief qualification for being sent to China was his knowledge of English, drew up the constitution of the Kuomintang, wrote its manifesto and suggested its organizational structure. He taught the Kuomintang how to spread effective propaganda by promising the masses redress of their grievances and improvement of their conditions. With Borodin came other Russian military and civilian experts, as well as a flow of arms and money to the Kuomintang. The transfusion of Soviet knowledge, experience, techniques and resources was to prove even more effective than Moscow had expected. Not only did it permit the Kuomintang to gain its further triumphs but it laid the organizational groundwork which later permitted the Kuomintang leadership under Chiang Kai-shek—after Sun Yat-sen's death—to defeat the Soviet design for China and for a time almost completely to destroy the Chinese Communist party. None of this was foreseen by the Moscow leaders, who even admitted the Kuomintang to the Communist International as a "sympathizer member."

In the mid-1920's the agreements and preparations of 1923–1924 bore rich fruit for a time. The Kuomintang grew stronger politically and militarily and after 1925 it rapidly extended its sway over China's territory, defeating the armies of some warlords and winning over others as its prospects for triumph became clearer. The Communists in the Kuomintang also gained greatly in these years. They dominated many of the lower Kuomintang party units and won great influence over the workers, peasants and students in the expanding areas of Kuomintang control. To Stalin in Moscow all seemed to be going well and according to plan, a conviction strengthened in him by Leon Trotsky's opposition to his China policy. To Trotsky, the correct policy in China was one which would have emphasized an independent Communist party, one following a line of strictly revolutionary practice based upon the organization of Chinese Soviets of workers and peasants. There were many Chinese Communists who shared Trotsky's misgivings and wanted to break with the Kuomintang. They knew that they were spreading Kuomintang propaganda and ideas, not Communist propaganda and ideas, while acting as Kuomintang agents. These Chinese Communists knew also that, for all their strength among the masses, they were very weak in the Kuomintang army, many of whose officers came from landowners' families and therefore looked with horror upon the prospect of peasant revolts and land seizures. But Stalin, confident of his own genius and determined to give no ground to Trotsky in the internal Kremlin power struggle, persevered in his pro-Kuomintang policy, time and again rebuffing Chinese Communist pleas for a change.

Within the Kuomintang there were also differences of opinion and misgivings on continued cooperation with the Communists. To an influential group of right wingers it seemed as though the Communists were taking over the Kuomintang. This group—known as the Western Hills group*—demanded expulsion of the Communists from the Kuomintang and dismissal of Borodin and all the other Russian advisers. The result was a Kuomintang split and the Western Hills group formed its own separate national organization. Much cleverer was Chiang Kai-shek. In words he praised the utility of the alliance with the Soviet Union and the advantages of having the Communists within the Kuomintang. But his real attitude became clear —for those with eyes to see—on March 20, 1926, when he arrested the Communist political commissars attached to his troops and put his Soviet advisers under house arrest. This put Canton under his firm control. This accomplished, he proceeded to make apologies and patch things up, but the power remained his. Two months later he rammed through a resolution barring Communists from all top

---

* They were named for the Western Hills near Peking, where the members met in December 1925 and formulated their policy.

Kuomintang posts and forbidding them to criticize Kuomintang doctrine. The mutterings of Communist discontent grew louder, but Stalin was deaf to them, and Borodin refused to give the Communists the Soviet arms they wanted to create their own military forces. Stalin was confident he would know when the proper time came for the break between Chiang and the Chinese Communists. Events were to prove Chiang Kai-shek the shrewder tactician.

The climax of this struggle came in April 1927 when Chiang's army stood at the gates of a Shanghai ruled by Communist-controlled workers. Moscow ordered that he be admitted to Shanghai unopposed, warning against any clashes and suggesting the workers hide their weapons. At dawn on April 12, Chiang's troops struck. They easily overcame the workers' resistance and then began a reign of terror against all Communists, real or imagined. This "purification movement" went on for many months, and its massacre of Communists and their sympathizers, particularly in Shanghai, Nanking and Canton, did much to break the substantial strength Chinese Communism had amassed in the great cities. The Communists preserved a position for a time in the so-called Wuhan (named for the Chinese cities of Wuchang, Hankow, and Hanyang) government, where they were allied with the left wing of the Kuomintang, but this blew up in June 1927 when Moscow ordered the Communists to back peasant land seizures, to "destroy the present unreliable generals," and oust the members of the Kuomintang Central Committee. Informed of these orders by the indiscretion of the Indian Communist Roy, the Wuhan leaders joined forces with Chiang Kai-shek and the break between the Kuomintang and Moscow became complete. Stalin's policy thus ended in a debacle. Borodin left China for Moscow in July 1927 and subsequent Communist efforts—such as the great rising in Canton the following December—were drowned in blood. By the end of 1928, Chiang controlled most of China and the Chinese Communists—the few who were

left—were a powerless, hunted fragment of a once powerful political force.

In Manchuria during the middle and late 1920's another Soviet-Chinese drama was being enacted, this one
over the Chinese Eastern Railroad. Moscow's 1924 treaty
with the Peking government and its Mukden Agreement
with the Manchurian administration of Marshal Chang
Tso-lin had provided for joint Sino-Soviet management
of the railroad as a commercial venture. Once this was
begun, irritations and disputes multiplied so that the
railroad was a continuing source of Sino-Soviet hostility.
To the Chinese it soon seemed that the new Soviet officials
were behaving exactly like the old Tsarist Russian officials
before 1917 and with the same basic purpose: to establish
Russian hegemony over the railroad zone and northern
Manchuria. The Chinese complained, with more than a
little justice, that the nominally equal control exercised
by Soviet and Chinese officials over the railroad was a
mockery, a façade hiding the reality of virtually unchecked
Soviet control over the line's day-by-day operations. The
Chinese felt, too, that the railroad was being looted by its
Soviet management in a variety of ways for the benefit of
the Soviet Union, of Russian workers on the line and of
the Communist cause. Most important, the Chinese felt
the Soviet control of the railroad was being employed as a
weapon to advance Soviet interests in China and to try to
affect the course of the military and political struggles
going on in North China in these years. In late 1925 and
early 1926, for example, the Soviet general manager Ivanov
tried to stop the transportation, without immediate cash
payment, of Chinese military forces on the railroad. To
Chang Tso-lin this seemed a transparent effort to impede
his military movements against the rebel General Kuo
Sung-lin who was widely suspected of being a Russian
puppet. In retaliation, Marshal Chang had Ivanov and
three other high Russian officials arrested, and for a time
the Chinese ran the railroad until the dispute was patched

up by a compromise formula. Soviet relations with Chang Tso-lin worsened further in April 1927. At that time the Manchurian warlord, then in control of Peking, raided the Soviet embassy, arrested Communist leaders there and seized many documents.* In retaliation, the Soviet government ordered its envoy in Peking and his staff home, though Soviet consuls and representatives remained in many other Chinese cities.

The twin disputes over management of the C.E.R. and the spread of Communist propaganda reached a crisis in mid-1929. Chinese police raided the Soviet consulate in Harbin, arrested numerous Soviet citizens there and seized documents which the police reported showed a Russian plot to secure the violent overthrow of the Nationalist government. In retaliation the Soviet government suspended the diplomatic immunity of Chinese diplomats on its territory. Finally, on July 10 and 11, the Chinese took over control of the railroad and its entire communications system. They arrested and deported the highest Russian managers of the C.E.R. and closed down various Soviet agencies in Manchuria as well as different organizations of the C.E.R.'s employees. Moscow's answer was to break off all diplomatic relations with China (except in Sinkiang, which was effectively independent of Chiang Kai-shek's regime) and to suspend all railroad communication between Russia and China.

This was the start of an undeclared, but at times very real and bloody, war between Russia and China over the next several months. A series of violent border clashes took place between the forces of both nations and Soviet planes bombed strategic points in Manchuria, while pro-

---

* The Peking police later published what it said were translations of the seized documents. This produced a tremendous stir because the published materials appeared to expose direct Soviet involvement in efforts to set up a Communist government in China, and use of Soviet diplomats in China to foster this end. Naturally the Soviet government denounced the published documents as forgeries, but they did have a great impact on Chinese public opinion, and it is likely many of them were authentic.

Soviet Outer Mongolian forces attacked in the region of Hailar. Military events in this war reached a climax in the autumn of 1929. In October combined Soviet sea, air and land forces destroyed the Chinese Sungari River fleet and captured Tungkiang. The following month Soviet land forces captured the cities of Manchouli and Chalainor after heavy fighting. China's military strength was clearly inadequate to cope with the Soviet forces, a fact the Manchurian authorities recognized in December when they agreed to the Khabarovsk Protocol. This document amounted to a complete surrender by the Chinese, since it provided for restoration of the original status of the C.E.R. before the Chinese takeover of the previous July. According to official Chinese reports, the struggle had cost China some 10,000 lives and about half a billion dollars in property loss.

The Soviet military success in Manchuria was accompanied, however, by political embarrassment. Even within the Communist movement, there were many who asked whether Russia's military moves to protect its hold on the C.E.R. were not simply in the old imperialist tradition and a far cry, in particular, from the spirit of the Karakhan Declarations. The Chinese Communist party's leadership dutifully supported Moscow in the dispute, advancing the slogan "Protect the Soviet Union." But more of a justification was needed. Hence the argument was advanced that the Soviet position in the railroad was needed to protect the line from being taken over by the imperialists and also to make it easier eventually to transfer the line to the Chinese proletariat when the Chinese revolution would be victorious. These arguments were to be hastily forgotten a few years later, however, when the Soviet Union decided that in its own interest it should transfer the railroad to an imperialist power, Japan.

Thus, at the end of the 1920's Moscow could look back on a mixed but not unproductive period of its Chinese policy. China's starry-eyed *naïveté* about the Soviet Union and its beneficent intentions toward China had been shattered. So, too, had been Moscow's hopes of gaining a Communist China as a satellite. But Outer Mongolia had again been detached from China and made a satellite, while in Manchuria much of the old Tsarist position had been regained, first by diplomacy in 1924 and then by force of arms in 1929. It was not a record to be sneered at.

CHAPTER VII

Russia, China and Japan in the 1930's

Fear of foreign attack dominated much of Soviet policy at home and abroad during the 1930's. The rising tides of Hitlerite military strength in Germany and Japanese conquest in Asia threatened to put Stalin's realm in a vise from which the Soviet Union might not be able to escape. At home, Stalin's response was a pitiless campaign to build Soviet military-economic power regardless of cost. In the Far East, his tactics went through intricate convolutions from appeasement of Japan at one extreme to undeclared war against Nipponese troops at the other. In the complex situation thus created, much of Stalin's China policy in this decade was a consequence of the needs created by his relations with Japan. The effort to use China in Russia's plans to resist Japan combined with the relative weakness of the Chinese Communists to make traditional Russian and Soviet hopes for the conquest of China of secondary importance during these years. The diversity of Stalin's tactics is indicated, however, by the fact that during this decade he surrendered the Russian position in Manchuria he had regained at such cost and effort in the 1920's, fought an undeclared war to keep Outer Mongolia under his wing and created a new Soviet satellite in China, the province of Sinkiang.

To create the vast Asian empire to which its militarists aspired, Japan had to conquer China, drive Russia away from the Pacific by seizing at least the Soviet Far East and evict Russia from its conquests in China. The easy

Soviet victory over the Chinese in Manchuria in late 1929 showed the ambitious men in Tokyo where the weakest point in their intended victims' defenses was located. In September 1931 the Japanese army struck at the Manchurian walled city of Mukden, opening an offensive which brought all Manchuria—including the Russian sphere surrounding the Chinese Eastern Railroad—under Japanese control. In March 1932 the Japanese created their puppet state of Manchukuo. This easy triumph produced a deep impression in Moscow, where the inferiority of Soviet military strength *vis-à-vis* the Japanese in the Far East was well understood.

Stalin's response was two-fold. Insofar as his propaganda apparatus—working through the Chinese Communists and other instruments—could do so, it sought to stimulate Chinese resistance to Japan. But for the Soviet Union itself, a policy of appeasement was decided upon. Soviet weakness at home was at the root of this policy. In the first half of the 1930's, it should be remembered, Russia was going through twin ordeals. Stalin was simultaneously carrying out the beginning stages of forced industrialization and trying to impose the hated collective farm system upon his recalcitrant peasants. A war with Japan at this juncture might have resulted in more than disastrous military consequences in the Far East. It might have shaken Communist power in Russia as deeply as, or even more deeply than, the Russo-Japanese War shook the Tsarist regime in 1905.

The policy of appeasement showed itself in many ways. Russia declared its strict neutrality in the conflict between China and Japan. It accepted the replacement of Nationalist China's officials on the Chinese Eastern Railroad by Manchukuoan puppets. And finally, under Japanese harassment of the railroad's operations, Moscow decided to sell its interest in the Chinese Eastern to Manchukuo and its Japanese masters. The offer to sell was made in mid-1933, and Russia asked 250,000,000 gold rubles, equivalent to 650,000,000 yen. Then began an involved series of negotiations, punctuated by bitter words and harsh pressures from both sides. But the Japanese held the upper hand since they controlled the territory through which the railroad ran and could hamper its operation in many ways, as they did. In March 1935 the deal was finally concluded. The railroad was sold to Manchukuo for 140,000,000 yen plus a Manchukuoan promise to assume the payment of the retirement allowances due the line's employees. This was a price less than one-third the amount Moscow had originally asked.

Bowing to superior Japanese force, Russia had given up a foothold in Manchuria whose attainment and retention had been a major goal of both Tsarist and Soviet policy for almost half a century. Soviet Foreign Minister Maxim Litvinov justified the Soviet decision to sell by saying: "In the building of the road in Manchuria, in foreign territory, the Tsarist government unquestionably was pursuing imperialist aims. After the October revolution the road lost the significance it had for the people of the Russian empire as an instrument of penetration."[1] This was a very different tune indeed from the one Moscow and the Communist International had sung less than four years earlier when the Soviet Union was willing to, and did, fight an undeclared war with China to retain the Chinese Eastern Railroad. *Izvestiya* in 1935 answered in a vein similar to Litvinov's when the Chinese government protested the sale as a violation of the 1924 Sino-Soviet Treaty which had permitted re-establishment of the Soviet position on the Chinese Eastern. But, despite the Chinese protest, Soviet relations with Chiang Kai-shek's regime were already improving slowly; diplomatic relations between the two countries had been resumed in December 1932.

Any hopes Moscow may have had that its retreat from Manchuria would satisfy Japanese appetites soon faded. Diffculties arose quickly along the border between Manchuria and Siberia. Since much of it was not clearly demarcated, border disputes and clashes broke out, some of them reaching the magnitude of actual battles. Alarmed by growing Soviet military strength in the Far East, Japan

demanded that Russia destroy the fortifications along the
border with Manchukuo and neutralize it. Moscow refused
the demand. It pointed out that the Trans-Siberian Railroad—the Soviet supply line to the Far East—ran very
close to the border in many places, and could therefore
easily be destroyed by a Japanese military blow if left
undefended. In turn, Japan turned down Soviet suggestions for a nonaggression pact between the two countries.
The rising tension was further intensified in November
1936 when Germany and Japan announced the Anti-
Comintern Pact. Nominally this was directed at the sub-
versive activities of the Communist International, and the
published portions of the pact did not even mention
the Soviet Union. But there could be little doubt in Moscow
that this was actually a Berlin-Tokyo alliance aimed at
encircling and defeating the Soviet Union.

Soviet-Japanese tension also climbed in the mid-1930's
because of differences over Outer Mongolia, a Soviet
satellite Tokyo schemed to detach from Moscow. Japanese occupation of Manchuria had brought Nippon's power
to the eastern border of Outer Mongolia, another poorly
demarcated boundary easily productive of territorial disputes and clashes. During 1933–1935 Japanese forces also
advanced deep into Inner Mongolia, putting them into a
position to exert pressure on Outer Mongolia from the
south as well as the east. In 1934 Manchukuo proposed a
mutual recognition agreement to the Outer Mongolian government in Ulan Bator (the city formerly known as
Urga). This agreement proposed to establish Manchukuoan
representation in Outer Mongolia and thus end the latter's
isolation from the rest of the world. Moscow could hardly
welcome this proposal. Its acceptance would have opened
the Ulan Bator government to possible Japanese penetration
and influence. Hence the Soviet Union saw to it that the
idea was rejected. Instead, the Soviet Union promised in-
formally to increase its direct military aid to Outer Mongolia in late 1934, just before the major battle over Lake
Bor Nor in January 1935 between Mongolian and Manchukuoan forces. Diplomatic negotiations following this

battle lasted many months during 1935, but failed to reach any agreement. The result was a new and increasingly frequent series of border clashes. With a Japanese attack upon Outer Mongolia apparently possible at any moment, Stalin announced publicly in February 1936 that the Soviet Union would come to the aid of Outer Mongolia if the Japanese should attack. Two months later it was revealed that Moscow and Ulan Bator had concluded a mutual assistance pact amounting to a military alliance. These moves all constituted an effective Soviet announcement that the period of Japanese appeasement was over. The story of the Chinese Eastern Railroad would not be repeated in Outer Mongolia. But the mutual assistance pact also made explicit what had been implicit but clear for many years: Outer Mongolia was a Soviet satellite and the 1924 Soviet promise to Peking to regard Outer Mongolia as part of China was long since dead. Chiang Kai-shek's government protested the 1936 treaty, pointing out that a Chinese province had no right to conclude an independent treaty with a foreign power. The protest was clearly only for the record, since Chiang had no power available to influence events in Outer Mongolia.

In Outer Mongolia, of course, the years between the early 1920's and the mid-1930's had been used to make the country completely dependent upon the Soviet Union. The power of the princes and lamas was smashed and the great bulk of their property taken away from them. During the early 1930's an effort was made to duplicate in Outer Mongolia the mass collectivization of agriculture that was taking place in the Soviet Union. But strong popular resistance and the difficulties encountered in trying to collectivize a mass of illiterate nomadic herdsmen forced a major retreat in 1932 and an end for a time to the collectivization efforts. The Soviet Union and its representatives in Outer Mongolia clearly dominated the area's economy and its foreign trade, however.

There was Soviet-Japanese competition also during the first half of the 1930's in a third major Chinese border area, Sinkiang. In this vast, thinly settled region of deserts, oases and mountains, most of the population consists of non-Chinese Moslem peoples—Kazakhs, Uigurs, Kirghiz, Uzbeks and others—closely related to the peoples of Soviet Central Asia. Japanese domination of Sinkiang thus would have posed an immediate and clear political threat to the Soviet position in the important areas immediately west of the Chinese border. The political, economic and military advantages of adding Sinkiang to the Soviet Union, or making it a satellite on the model of Outer Mongolia, must also have occurred to the Soviet leaders. Certainly their policy in the 1930's gave them a dominant position in Sinkiang that went far beyond the needs of defense against the Japanese threat.

Shrewd maneuvering by the Chinese governor of Sinkiang in the decade following the Bolshevik Revolution had prevented anything beyond restoration of the old Russian major trading presence in the area. Given the disorders which afflicted China proper during the 1920's, Sinkiang during that period enjoyed almost independent relations with the Soviet Union. Thus in 1927, when Chinese-Soviet relations were broken off, Sinkiang's consul general in the Soviet city of Semipalatinsk issued a public declaration that his office "has nothing in common with Central China. . . . This consulate is dependent upon Western China, which does not wish, in any case, to sever its friendship with the U.S.S.R."[2]

Two events at the beginning of the 1930's set the stage for the tremendous increase of Soviet influence which took place in Sinkiang during that decade. One was the completion of the Turkestan-Siberian Railroad (Turksib) connecting the Trans-Siberian Railroad with the major cities of Soviet Central Asia, including several very close to the Sinkiang border and lying on the main trade routes into the area. This immediately fortified the already great commercial advantages the Soviet Union enjoyed *vis-à-vis* Sinkiang. The second development was the outbreak of a major Moslem revolt against the Chinese governor of Sinkiang, Chin Shu-jen. This revolt, led by the brilliant

General Ma Chung-ying, derived its strength from the
real grievances of Sinkiang's Moslem majority against
the exploitative and corrupt Chinese rule, but there is
evidence that General Ma's forces had at least unofficial
Japanese support and he had Japanese agents in his
entourage. In this situation Governor Chin turned to
Moscow for support, not even bothering to inform the
Chiang Kai-shek regime of what he was doing. Apparently in return for Soviet promises of military assistance, he gave Soviet economic penetration of Sinkiang
vast new scope in a secret trade agreement signed in
October 1931. Customs duties on Soviet goods were reduced. Telegraph and radio communications facilities were
set up under nominally joint Sinkiang-Soviet—but actually
Soviet—auspices. Soviet commercial representatives were
given freedom of movement in the province, and eight
Soviet trade agencies were permitted to open their doors
in Sinkiang's most important communities.

Governor Chin proved to be inadequate to deal with the
thorny problems before him, and he fled the province in
April 1933 when a mutiny broke out among White Russian troops in his forces. His successor, General Sheng
Shih-tsai, was a remarkable figure who managed to rule
for roughly a decade, skillfully riding the very turbulent
and complex political currents that swept Sinkiang.
General Sheng was in effect a Marxist warlord who
revolutionized life in the province and preserved Chinese
suzerainty with vast Soviet help. In response to Sheng's
appeal for assistance against General Ma's Moslem forces,
Moscow sent troops and planes into Sinkiang, and these
guaranteed Sheng's victory in 1934. Alexander Barmine,
a Soviet official who later defected to the West, described
what happened as he saw it from his position as head of
the Soviet organization in charge of secret military de-
liveries abroad:

The Politburo ordered two brigades of G.P.U. troops
with air units of the Red Army to clear the roads and
liquidate the rebellion. Meanwhile, on the order of the

Politburo, we shipped a number of planes and bombs to the borders of Sinkiang. There they were stuck for some time, as the road to Urumchi . . . was blocked by the rebels. Finally the command of the Red Army Air Force operating there took charge of this shipment. They delivered our cargoes, consigned to the governor, by dropping bombs on the rebel forces gathered round the capital, and by landing the planes right on the airfield of the besieged fortress. I was instructed to send the bill for the bombs, as well as the other goods, to the governor.[3]

Moscow's continued suspicion of General Sheng was evidenced after the victory when the defeated General Ma was given political asylum in the Soviet Union. His presence there gave Stalin an alternative Sinkiang leader, should Sheng break with the Soviet Union. This threat, plus Sheng's Marxist beliefs and his dependence upon the Soviet Union for economic and military aid, resulted in a Sinkiang foreign policy based upon "anti-imperialism" and "pro-Sovietism." Russian advisers swarmed into Sinkiang. Anti-Soviet elements were purged and a Sinkiang equivalent of the Soviet secret police was set up. Sinkiang, in short, became virtually a Soviet colony during the middle and late 1930's. General Sheng himself was ordered by Stalin to join, and did join, the Communist party of the Soviet Union. At the same time, however, Sinkiang made important strides in economic development and in provision of educational and medical facilities to the population. But in name Sinkiang remained a part of China, and events after 1937 showed that this had more than merely juridical importance.

We have seen that between 1930 and 1936 the Soviet Union, forced out of its major position in Manchuria and compelled to announce that it would go to war to defend its hold in Outer Mongolia against Japan, had established a major new position of political, economic and military dominance in Sinkiang. We must now turn to a fourth thread of the complex story of Soviet-Chinese relations in this period: the Chinese Communists whom we left defeated in the major cities by Chiang Kai-shek and his Kuomintang. Moscow could not admit that Stalin's tactics in China had brought disaster; it refused to admit defeat. Stalin blamed setbacks on the mistakes of Chinese Communist leaders and on the succession of Comintern representatives who had advised them. He spurred what remained of the Chinese Communist party on to raise armed revolution in the cities. To make sure that the Chinese Communist party remained loyal to him and followed his instructions, Stalin had that party's Sixth Congress held in Moscow in July 1928. But this did not help. Though Stalin purged Chinese party leaders and changed Comintern agents, the Chinese Communist party proved impotent against the forces of Chiang Kai-shek in the great cities—the centers of the Chinese proletariat—in the late 1920's and early 1930's. A measure of Moscow's desperation, as defeat followed defeat, was the installation in January 1931 of the so-called "Returned Students Clique" into the leadership of the Chinese party. These "callow Bolsheviks," as their opponents called them, were a group of young men who had studied at Moscow's Sun Yat-sen Academy and who had little practical knowledge of China. Their chief merit was their high status with the Comintern agent for China, the Russian Pavel Mif, who was the real ruler of what remained of the Chinese Communist party apparatus. Their elevation to the leadership is important for our purposes only because, as Charles B. McLane has pointed out, the meeting at which they were installed "is the last identifiable instance of outright Soviet intervention in the internal affairs of the Chinese Communist party."[4] (We shall see later that in the early 1960's evidence of Soviet intervention in Chinese Communist party internal affairs in 1959 became available.) But all this represented a dead end for Chinese Communism. Its real future, history was to show, was being prepared in China's vast rural areas.

The path that was to lead to a Communist China was first broken by Mao Tse-tung in 1927 when he turned to the rural areas of South China and began organizing peasant soviets. In the next few years he worked out in practice the basic elements that were to lead to victory: the seizure of fixed territorial bases; the winning of peasant support by distributing the land of the richest peasants and drastically easing the burdens imposed by rural money lenders; the setting up of a Red Army which engaged in hit-and-run guerrilla warfare against numerically superior government forces; and tight Communist party control over and indoctrination of the population of the areas he controlled. Moscow was pleased and excited at the first news of the Chinese soviets. Initially it thought of these rural beginnings as merely a helpful sideshow to the main effort, which it thought must be made in the great cities. But as the soviet areas expanded in late 1929 and 1930, Moscow began to realize the full potentialities of this movement. It ordered the formation of a Chinese Soviet Republic on the Russian model. This new government was proclaimed at the First Congress of Chinese Soviets in Juikin, Kiangsi Province, in November 1931. Mao Tse-tung, named chairman of this new "republic," was now in fact the main leader of Chinese Communism, though he did not receive full, unchallenged recognition of his leadership until 1935.

During the next few years a bitter struggle was waged between Mao Tse-tung's forces and those of the Chiang Kai-shek regime. To Chiang, the task of eradicating these new centers of Communist power had top priority even over the struggle against Japan, and he sent army after army against the Communist military strength. The Communists for their part regarded the Kuomintang and the Japanese equally as their enemies, and called for war against both. In early 1933, after four major efforts by Chiang Kai-shek's troops had failed to liquidate the soviet areas, the Chinese Communists controlled some thirty districts in the Kiangsi, Fukien and Chekiang provinces of South China, in the areas north and northeast of Canton. The Chinese Red Army had about 300,000 men, many of them equipped with rifles and other weapons captured

from the Kuomintang troops. But by October 1934 a new
major campaign by Chiang Kai-shek—one in which full
account had been taken of all the guerrilla stratagems
Mao Tse-tung's forces had used earlier—forced the Chinese Communists to give up their South China base and to
begin the epic in their history known as the Long March.
Even anti-Communists grant that this trek of more than
5,000 miles was a saga of courage, discipline and faithful-
ness with few analogues in history. Harried by Chiang's
troops much of the way, forced to climb major mountain
ranges and to ford great rivers, often short of food and, in
winter, suffering from extreme cold, the Chinese Communists had enormous losses during this hegira. Fewer than a
third of the 100,000 men who had begun the trek completed it. Those who survived the ravages of battle, disease, hunger, cold and exposure finally ended their journey
in October 1935 at the other end of China, in northern
Shensi Province. They were now entrenched in one of the
poorest, most primitive areas of China, in a hilly region
whose million and a half peasants—almost all illiterate
—barely raised enough food for themselves, let alone for
the army of 20,000–30,000 Mao Tse-tung had led there.

It is uncertain how much knowledge of, and control
over, Mao Tse-tung's activities Moscow enjoyed during
these years, particularly during the difficult time of the
Long March. At the very beginning of this period Moscow was certainly poorly informed. The official organ of
the Comintern, the *International Press Correspondence*
or *Imprecorr,* printed a long obituary of Mao Tse-tung in
March 1930, reporting he had died of consumption. Three
months later, at a Soviet Communist party congress, Stalin
revealed he was not clear about the situation. He referred
to reports of a Soviet government in China, and added: "I
think that if this is true, there is nothing surprising about
it."[5] Soviet information about the rural centers of Chinese
Communist power and liaison with them improved later.
But given the complex and difficult situations the Chinese
Communists often found themselves in, and the communications problems which existed, there seems little likelihood

that Moscow can have had the same close and unchallenged control in the 1930's that it had enjoyed in the 1920's.

In the first half of the 1930's, the Chinese Communists looked upon both the Japanese and Chiang Kai-shek's Kuomintang as their mortal enemies. They took it for granted that a struggle to the death must take place between the two main Chinese forces of that time and attacked Chiang Kai-shek frequently as a lackey of Japanese imperialism. But by 1935 Stalin saw clearly the danger posed to the Soviet Union by the rise of Hitler's power in Germany and the menace of advancing Japanese strength east and south of the Soviet position in Asia. His response, made clear in August 1935 when the Seventh Congress of the Communist International met in Moscow, was the decision to make the fight against fascism and imperialism the paramount goal of Communist parties everywhere, to make the "united front" tactic central everywhere and to have Communists unite with all possible forces that could help stem the rising power of Germany, Italy and Japan. In China this global decision meant that the Chinese Communists must seek a united front with Chiang Kai-shek, their hated enemy who had caused the death of thousands of Communists. Such a sharp turn in policy could not help but cause sharp disillusionment and bitterness among many of Mao's followers, as well as attempted opposition. An important factor, however, helped make this major policy reversal palatable for many party members. This was the fact that the new center of Chinese Communist strength in Shensi Province was directly in the path of Japanese expansion. In deciding to join forces with Chiang Kai-shek against Japan, Mao was not only following Moscow's instructions but also seeking to defend his own territorial base against an enemy even more formidable militarily than Chiang. But how was unity to be attained with a Chiang Kai-shek who still considered the Chinese Communists his enemies, sought to destroy their forces and feared and fought Russian designs in China?

Two developments, one in December 1936 and the

second in July 1937, solved the problem. As a result of these events there was established both a Kuomintang–Chinese Communist united front against Japan, and a Chiang Kai-shek–Stalin military assistance agreement. In the space of little more than a decade, Kuomintang-Soviet relations had turned through a complete circle of 360 degrees.

The first event was the Sian crisis at the end of 1936. Visiting that city to put more heart into troops slated to begin a new drive against the Communists, Chiang Kai-shek was arrested by his own local commanders and presented with a list of eight demands. These amounted to a demand for an end to the civil war and a union of the Kuomintang and Chinese Communist forces for war against Japan. Moscow immediately made clear through its press that it considered the arrest a major blow against the struggle to unify China against Japan. The Chinese Communists joined the negotiations in Sian and helped substantially in the arrangements which finally permitted Chiang to return unharmed to his capital in Nanking. Chou En-lai, the chief Communist representative at Sian, thus provided substantial evidence of the sincerity of the Communists' desire to cooperate with Chiang. But the Kuomintang was by no means convinced that unity would be in its best interests or anything but a Trojan Horse technique.

The second event was the outbreak of full-fledged war between China and Japan in July 1937. Beginning at the Marco Polo Bridge on the outskirts of Peking, fighting soon spread to Tientsin, Shanghai and other centers. Japanese planes bombed the capital at Nanking. Chiang Kai-shek's efforts to delay or avoid all-out war with Japan now came to an end. A war began that was to last eight years and was ultimately to bring both the United States and Russia into conflict with Japan.

The war acted as a catalyst, bringing to fruition negotiations that had been going on for many months both between Chiang Kai-shek and Stalin and between the Kuomintang and the Chinese Communists. On August 21,

1937 the Chinese and Soviet governments signed a nonaggression pact whose practical effect was to pledge the Soviet government not to help Japan or to do anything which might help Japan, though Japan was not mentioned by name. The Soviet press at the same time was making clear Moscow's sympathy with and admiration of the Chinese resistance to the Japanese. A month later, on September 22, 1937, the Chinese Communist party issued a manifesto pledging itself to strive for the realization of Sun Yat-sen's Three People's Principles. This document announced the end of the party's effort to overthrow the Kuomintang regime by force, as well as promising an end to confiscation of land from landlords. The same manifesto abolished the Chinese Soviet Republic and announced that the Red Army had become a National Revolutionary Army under the control of the Military Affairs Commission of the National government. Chiang Kai-shek the next day hailed the Chinese Communist manifesto as "an outstanding instance of the triumph of national sentiment over every other consideration." A united front against Japan had come into being.

Moscow was the immediate beneficiary of the outbreak of the Chinese-Japanese War. The conflict occupied Japanese forces which might otherwise have been turned against the Soviet Union, and the fiercer the fighting the less likely was a Japanese attack against Soviet territory. The war also ended the possibility of Chaing Kai-shek making a deal with the Japanese, joining the anti-Comintern alliance and adding his forces to the German-Japanese bloc against the Soviet Union. Thus Moscow had every incentive to help the Chinese against the Japanese. The force of this incentive was increased by actual fighting between Soviet and Japanese forces. During July and August of 1938 bitter fighting between the two took place on the border at Chang-kufeng Hill near Posyet Bay not far from Vladivostok. Several hundred were dead or wounded before the fighting, and the border dispute, ended. Even more serious was the fighting on the Manchurian-Mongolian border. The battle there in the Nomonhan area pitted a mixed Mongolian-Soviet army against Japanese forces and resulted in thousands of casualties between May and September 1939. Russia effectively won both these tests of military strength on borders it had determined to defend. It seems reasonable to suppose that there would have been more such conflicts, and some might have ended differently, if so much of the Japanese strength had not been tied up in China proper.

The help the Soviet government gave China during the late 1930's was of several kinds. Soviet exports to Japan dropped precipitously. The Soviet delegate to the League of Nations spoke up frequently in that body for international condemnation of the Japanese aggression against China and for League of Nations moral and material assistance to China. But most important was the flow of Soviet arms, planes, munitions and military personnel to China from late 1937 on, a flow which halted only when Germany attacked the Soviet Union in June 1941.

At this point we must shift our attention to Sinkiang, the back door to China, which became the main channel for the flow of Soviet military and economic aid to Chiang Kai-shek during the late 1930's. We noted the Soviet military aid to Sheng Shih-tsai earlier in that decade which had enabled him to control Sinkiang while opening the door wide to Soviet penetration. In the spring of 1937 Sheng faced another threat to his position from Moslem forces under General Ma Hu-shan, brother-in-law of the leader of the earlier rebellion. Once again Sheng appealed to Moscow and more than 5,000 troops, including an air unit and an armored regiment, responded to his call. Once again Soviet troops intervened on a major scale in a purely internal Chinese matter. Their intervention was successful, and this time many of the Soviet troops remained. Thus arose a strange situation in which a Chinese area existed virtually independent of the central Chinese government and garrisoned by Soviet troops; yet in these years this area played a key role in making possible continued Chinese resistance to the Japanese. Moreover, Sinkiang in this period provided a route for communication between the Chinese Communist leadership at Yenan and Moscow, a route Moscow used to forward money and presumably advice to Yenan. Also Moscow sent Chinese Communists, including a brother of Mao Tse-tung, to Sinkiang, men who soon occupied key positions in Sheng's regime. Soviet influence in Sinkiang rose sharply in the years that followed, particularly as the competitive British economic influence was driven out by a combination of government order and Soviet cut-price competition. Yet Stalin was careful not to turn Sinkiang over to the Chinese Communists, a policy made dramatically clear when he refused to let Sheng join the Chinese Communist party and ordered him to join the Russian party instead. It is hard to avoid the conclusion that Stalin saw Sinkiang's future in terms of a much closer tie to the Soviet Union than to China, even to a China that might eventually be ruled by Communists.

At first Soviet supplies were delivered by sea, traveling the long route from Odessa to Canton, but this channel was closed off when the Japanese occupied Canton in late 1938. This closing of the sea access to Nationalist China had been anticipated and all through 1938 hundreds of thousands of coolies labored to build a road from Tarbagatai on the Sinkiang border with Russia across some 3,000 miles to Chungking. Trucks, camels and assorted pack animals were used to move supplies over this long and difficult route. Roughly $300,000,000 in Soviet credits were given Chiang Kai-shek's regime to finance these deliveries during 1938–1940. Of key importance in the varied aid China received were hundreds of Soviet planes, Soviet fliers to fly them and Soviet instructors to train Chinese pilots. An incidental benefit to the Soviet Union was the fact that hundreds of its pilots thus received combat training under actual combat conditions. A high level Soviet military mission under General Cherepanov assisted the Nationalist government and Russian advisers were attached to many of the Chinese armies. At Urumchi, capital of Sinkiang, the Russians set up a plant to